HEALTH CARE REFORM

Learning from International
Experience

EDITED BY

Chris Ham

Open University Press
Buckingham · Philadelphia

To Ioanna, Alex, Jessie and Matthew

Open University Press
Celtic Court
22 Ballmoor
Buckingham
MK18 1XW

and
1900 Frost Road, Suite 101
Bristol, PA 19007, USA

First Published 1997
Reprinted 1998

A catalogue record of this book is available from the British Library

ISBN 0 335 19889 9 (pb)   0 335 19890 2 (hb)

Library of Congress Cataloging-in-Publication Data
Ham, Christopher
    Health care reform: learning from international experience/Chris
Ham.
        p.   cm. — (State of health series)
    Includes bibliographical references and index.
    ISBN 0-335-19889-9 (pbk)   ISBN 0-335-19890-2 (hard)
    1. Health care reform—Europe.   2. Health care reform—United
States.   3. Medical care—Europe—Finance.   4. Medical care—United
States—Finance.   5. Medical policy—Europe.   6. Medical policy—
United States.   7. Insurance, Health—Europe.   8. Insurance,
Health—United States.   I. Title.   II. Series.
RA410.55.E85H35   1997
362.1'094—dc21   96-52124
                                                                                        CIP

Typeset by Type Study, Scarborough
Printed in Great Britain by St Edmundsbury Press,
Bury St Edmunds, Suffolk

CONTENTS

SERIES EDITOR'S INTRODUCTION

Health services in many developed countries have come under critical scrutiny in recent years. In part this is because of increasing expenditure, much of it funded from public sources, and the pressure this has put on governments seeking to control public spending. Also important has been the perception that resources allocated to health services are not always deployed in an optimal fashion. Thus at a time when the scope for increasing expenditure is extremely limited, there is a need to search for ways of using existing budgets more efficiently. A further concern has been the desire to ensure access to health care of various groups on an equitable basis. In some countries this has been linked to a wish to enhance patient choice and to make service providers more responsive to patients as 'consumers'.

Underlying these specific concerns are a number of more fundamental developments which have a significant bearing on the performance of health services. Three are worth highlighting. First, there are demographic changes, including the ageing population and the decline in the proportion of the population of working age. These changes will both increase the demand for health care and at the same time limit the ability of health services to respond to this demand.

Second, advances in medical science will also give rise to new demands within the health services. These advances cover a range of possibilities, including innovations in surgery, drug therapy, screening and diagnosis. The pace of innovation is likely to quicken as the end of the century approaches, with significant implications for the funding and provision of services.

Third, public expectations of health services are rising as those who use services demand higher standards of care. In part, this is stimulated by developments within the health service, including the availability of new technology. More fundamentally, it stems from the emergence of a more educated and informed population, in which people are accustomed to being treated as consumers rather than patients.

Against this background, policymakers in a number of countries are reviewing the future of health services. Those countries which have traditionally relied on a market in health care are making greater use of regulation and planning. Equally, those countries which have traditionally relied on regulation and planning are moving towards a more competitive approach. In no country is there complete satisfaction with existing methods of financing and delivery, and everywhere there is a search for new policy instruments.

The aim of this series is to contribute to debate about the future of health services through an analysis of major issues in health policy. These issues have been chosen because they are both of current interest and of enduring importance. The series is intended to be accessible to students and informed lay readers as well as to specialists working in this field. The aim is to go beyond a textbook approach to health policy analysis and to encourage authors to move debate about their issue forward. In this sense, each book presents a summary of current research and thinking, and an exploration of future policy directions.

Professor Chris Ham
Director of Health Services Management Centre
University of Birmingham

ACKNOWLEDGEMENTS

In the last 10 years my work has focused on two main issues: first, the implementation of the reforms to the United Kingdom national health service (NHS) initiated by the Thatcher government in 1989; and second, the parallel process of health care reform in a number of countries outside the United Kingdom. This book brings these interests together. In so doing, it draws on a wide range of projects with which I have been involved in the last decade. My own chapters in the book, as demonstrated by the references, seek to pull together ideas from a number of publications. They are also informed by participation in international meetings and networks of various kinds. The discussions at these meetings, both formal and informal, have shaped my thinking about the content and process of reform. Wherever possible, this influence is acknowledged in the text, but often the debates that have taken place – with practitioners as well as academics – have had a more subtle effect, making it difficult to attribute their influence in a conventional manner. For this reason I would like to acknowledge here the importance of these discussions and the benefit I have gained from collaboration with Mats Brommels, Johan Calltorp, Aad de Roo, and Richard Saltman among many others.

As editor, my thanks go first to my co-authors. Each has responded positively to my requests and this book would quite simply not have been possible without their enthusiastic involvement. Next I would like to acknowledge the generous support offered by Glaxo Wellcome which provided an educational grant to enable the contributors to attend a seminar in Birmingham on which this book is based. At the Health Services Management Centre, Anne van der Salm and Sarah Stewart helped greatly in the process of translating the conference papers into book form as the manuscript went through successive drafts, often meeting tight deadlines in the process. I would like to thank too Elsevier Science for permission to use a paper originally published in 1996 in *Health Policy*, 35: 279–92 in a slightly amended version as Chapter 3, and for permission to reproduce a figure from *Social Science and Medicine* as Figure 1.5. I would also like to acknowledge permission granted by the BMJ Publishing Group, the King's Fund and the Organisation for Economic Cooperation and Development (OECD) to reproduce figures as indicated in the text. Finally, this book is dedicated to my family who once more have had to put up with the intrusions into family life which writing and editing inevitably involve. Any errors are of course my responsibility.

LIST OF CONTRIBUTORS

Reinhard Busse is a Doctor of Medicine and Master of Public Health in the Department of Epidemiology and Social Medicine at the Centre of Public Health, Hannover.

Chris Ham is Professor of Health Policy and Management and Director of the Health Services Management Centre at the University of Birmingham.

Bradford Kirkman-Liff is Professor at the Arizona State College of Business at Tempe, Arizona.

Clas Rehnberg is Assistant Professor at the Centre for Health Economics at the Stockholm School of Economics.

Friedrich Wilhelm Schwartz is Professor in the Department of Epidemiology and Social Medicine at the Centre of Public Health, Hannover.

Wynand van de Ven is Professor of Health Insurance in the Department of Health Policy at Erasmus University, Rotterdam.

LIST OF ABBREVIATIONS

AMA	American Medical Association
EDI	electronic data interchange
EU	European Union
GDP	gross domestic product
GP	general practitioner
HA	health authority
HMO	health maintenance organization
NHI	national health insurance
NHS	national health service
OECD	Organisation for Economic Cooperation and Development
PAC	Political Action Committee
SHA	special health authority
WHO	World Health Organization

1

THE BACKGROUND
Chris Ham

Health care reform is in fashion internationally. Under continuing pressure to contain costs, increase efficiency, and raise service standards, health policy makers have introduced a range of changes to health care in the quest for improved performance. Various studies have described the reforms that have been pursued and have attempted to analyse their effects.[1] These studies confirm that almost everywhere there is dissatisfaction with existing methods of financing and delivery and a search for new policy instruments. At the same time, it is clear that there are no quick fix solutions to the challenges faced by the health care systems of developed countries. All the more reason therefore to evaluate the impact of different reform strategies and to ensure that the results are disseminated in order to inform future policy initiatives.

This book is a contribution to that process. It seeks to promote learning about health care reform by reviewing experiences in five countries whose health care systems have undergone significant change in recent years. These countries are the United States, the Netherlands, Sweden, the United Kingdom and Germany. The reasons for selecting these countries is that they illustrate the approach taken to reform in systems with quite different methods of financing and delivery. The United States relies mainly on private funding and private provision and has used competition to increase efficiency and promote choice for patients. In contrast, the United Kingdom and Sweden pay for health care mainly out of taxation with a large measure of public ownership of hospitals and public employment of staff. A different approach is found in the Netherlands and Germany where social insurance is the predominant method of funding and where there is a mixed economy of public and private providers.

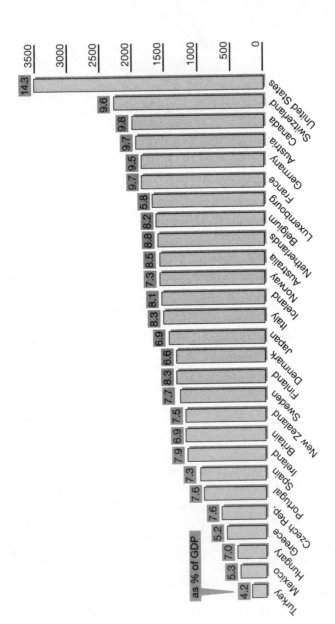

Figure 1.1 Health spending per person, 1994 ($ at purchasing-power parity)
Source: OECD (1996)

Health Care Reform: Learning from International Experience was conceived in part as a successor volume to *Health Check*, a study published in 1990 which reviewed the performance of health services in a number of countries to extract lessons for the United Kingdom.[2] Although most of the authors of this book did not contribute to *Health Check*, nevertheless there is a large measure of continuity between the two volumes. As we noted in 1990, there are some clear lessons from international experience. These include the weaknesses of private insurance as the main form of health service financing; the need to use either social insurance or tax funding to ensure equity and access in health care; and the existence of common problems in the delivery of health care almost regardless of the method and level of funding. What has changed in the intervening seven years is that there is much greater experience of the reforms that have been introduced to tackle these problems.

The core of the book comprises chapters written by experts in each of these countries about the reforms that have been pursued and their impact. The chapters were originally presented as papers at a seminar held at the Health Services Management Centre at the University of Birmingham in September 1995. They have since been updated to take into account more recent developments and in the light of the authors having heard the presentations of their co-authors. This chapter provides an introduction to the book by reviewing variations in health service financing and delivery in the developed world and the main themes in health care reform. The concluding chapter draws together the different strands from the country chapters and seeks to summarize and review the emerging themes. An attempt is made to go beyond the country chapters to identify the key lessons that have emerged as well as to highlight areas of continuing uncertainty. As such the book is intended to be of use to policy makers and to teachers of health policy and their students.

THE CONTEXT

There are wide differences between developed countries in both the volume and methods of health services financing. As Figure 1.1 shows, the proportion of GDP spent on health services in the OECD countries in 1994 ranged from 4.2 per cent in Turkey to 14.3 per cent in the United States.[3] The average for all OECD countries in that year was just under 8 per cent. A number of studies have

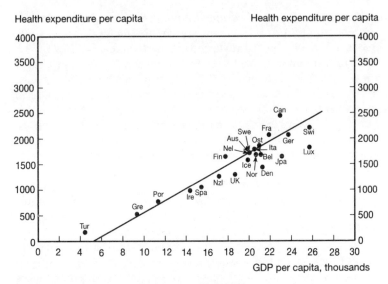

Figure 1.2   Health spending versus GDP, 1992
Source: OECD (1995). Reproduced by permission of the OECD.
Note: Both health expenditures and GDPs are compared using GDP purchasing power parities.

demonstrated that there is a close relationship between the level of national income in a country and the volume of expenditure on health care. This is illustrated in Figure 1.2.[4] As a general rule, rich countries spend a higher proportion of GDP on health care than poor countries. In most OECD countries, public funding accounts for around three-quarters of total health services expenditure. The United States is the main exception with less than half of health care spending being classified as public.

As Maxwell has argued, although there are almost endless variations in the pattern of health care financing, a number of methods have come to predominate (see Figure 1.3).[5] While all countries rely on a mixture of funding sources, three broad approaches can be identified. First, there is public finance based on taxation. This is the preferred approach in the Nordic countries, the United Kingdom, New Zealand, Italy and Spain and it is often referred to as the Beveridge model. Second, there is public finance based on compulsory social insurance. This is the method used in countries like Germany, the Netherlands, France and Belgium, and is usually described as the Bismarck model. Third, there is private finance based on voluntary insurance, as is found in the United States.

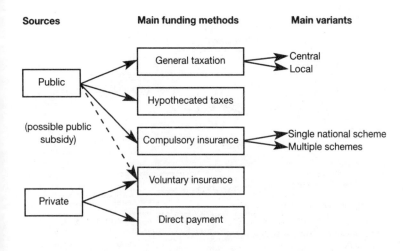

Figure 1.3   Methods of financing
Source: Maxwell (1988). Reproduced by kind permission of the BMJ Publishing Group.

Experience suggests that there are inherent weaknesses in using voluntary insurance as the main method of financing health services. These include the uncertainty and risks involved in insuring against ill health; the existence of moral hazard for both users and providers, leading to overutilization and inappropriate use of services; an incentive for insurers to select risks and to engage in cream skimming of patients; the difficulty of ensuring universal coverage and equitable access to health care of different groups in the population; and the high level of administrative costs. It is because of these market failures that governments have intervened in most developed countries to legislate either for single payer tax financing or compulsory social insurance. The move towards universal population coverage helps to explain the increase in health service spending over time and the fact that the public share of total health services expenditure comprises the biggest element in the health service budget in nearly all OECD countries.

Analysis of expenditure patterns shows that the rate of increase in spending was generally slower in the 1980s than the 1960s and 1970s.[6] This reflects steps taken in response to the oil crisis in the 1970s when governments in all OECD countries acted to contain the growth of public expenditure. Various measures were taken in pursuit of this objective including the use of prospective global

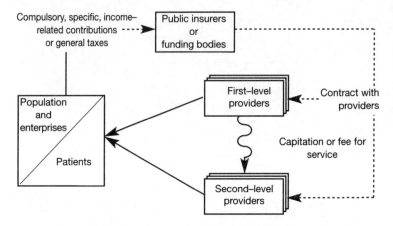

Figure 1.4a   Compulsory insurance with insurer/provider contracts
Source: OECD (1992). Reproduced by permission of the OECD.

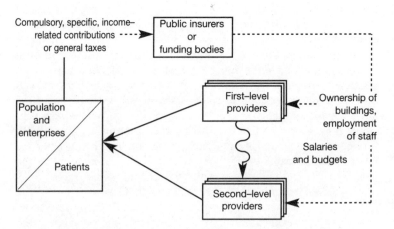

Figure 1.4b   Compulsory insurance with integration between insurance and provision
Source: OECD (1992). Reproduced by permission of the OECD.

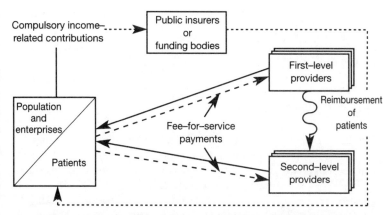

Figure 1.4c Compulsory insurance with reimbursement of patients
Source: OECD (1992). Reproduced by permission of the OECD.

budgets for hospitals, controls over hospital building and the acquisition of medical equipment, limits on doctors' fees and incomes, and restrictions on the numbers undertaking education and training for health service work. These measures were largely successful with the consequence that the share of total health expenditure deriving from public sources fell in many countries during the 1980s. This is because governments have a greater capacity to control public spending on health care than private expenditure, and it has also resulted from moves to increase cost sharing through the use of patient charges and co-payments. Against this, some European countries took steps to extend the scope of public financing and calls to privatize health service funding were on the whole not heeded in the 1980s.[7]

Much more important than the privatization of health service funding was the shift from an integrated model of health service finance and provision to a contract model (see Figure 1.4).[8] The United Kingdom national health service has traditionally been run on integrated lines, combining public finance with public ownership of hospitals and salaried employment of doctors. The public contract model, by contrast, involves insurers ensuring that services are available to patients by negotiating contracts with independent providers. This is the system that exists in Germany where sickness funds contract with hospitals and doctors on behalf of their members. A third approach is represented by the public reimbursement model in which patients are reimbursed for the costs of their care by insurers but where no contracts exist between insurers and providers. Both the Belgian and French systems have been run in this way.

RECENT REFORMS

The shift from the integrated to the contract model was stimulated by a move in the second half of the 1980s to supplement policies to contain costs at the macro level with initiatives to increase efficiency and enhance responsiveness to service users at the micro level. A wide range of policy instruments were used in pursuit of these objectives.[9] First, there was interest in some countries in introducing market-like mechanisms into the health services. In part, this was motivated by disillusion with planning as a tool for increasing efficiency and responsiveness, and in part it was a response to the election of governments with an ideological preference for markets over bureaucracies. One of the earliest attempts to promote competition was the Dekker report of 1987[10] in the Netherlands and this was quickly followed by moves to introduce competition in the United Kingdom, New Zealand and Sweden. Similar ideas have either been debated or are being implemented in Finland, Germany, Italy and Spain. The interest in markets led to the separation of purchaser and provider responsibilities in integrated systems and explains the move towards the contract model.

Second, there was a concern to strengthen the management of health services. The aim here was to reduce variations in performance and to introduce a stronger customer orientation. The latter included offering patients greater choice, improving access by reducing waiting lists, and increasing the quality of care. The Griffiths report of 1983[11] in the United Kingdom exemplified this approach and its recommendations were echoed elsewhere. By drawing on ideas from successful businesses, health policy makers sought to improve information systems, involve doctors, nurses and other staff in management, and devolve responsibility for management to hospitals and units within hospitals.

In some countries there was a move too to examine how services that were previously provided in the public sector could be supplied by private companies under contract to the public sector. This reflected trends in a number of major industries to restructure their operations away from vertical integration to contracting with suppliers. The policy of strengthening management also involved the appointment of managers to run hospitals and other facilities in a more professional fashion. The fact that these managers were often employed on short-term contracts and received performance related pay only served to sharpen the incentive for them to deliver. Italy was one of those countries that sought to strengthen hospital management, including running some hospitals on a self-governing basis, and there were parallel developments in Denmark.

Third, there was interest in making use of budgetary incentives as a way of improving performance. A key factor here was recognition that prospective global budgets were effective in containing expenditure but offered little or no incentive to those running hospitals to increase their efficiency or to provide services that were attractive to users. Policy makers therefore explored ways of combining cost control with payment systems that rewarded desired improvements in performance. This was illustrated by the interest shown in Portugal and Sweden in diagnosis related group reimbursements for hospitals. In parallel, changes were made to doctors' fee schedules both as a means of limiting expenditure growth and of encouraging (or discouraging) certain practice patterns. An example from Germany was the attempt to control expenditure on pharmaceuticals by making doctors responsible for spending over a specified limit. Another kind of budgetary incentive was the use of patient charges or co-payments to moderate demand. Virtually all countries use cost sharing in some form, most notably for pharmaceuticals and dental care, although it was not a major plank of health service reform.

One of the most notable innovations in the use of incentives was the general practitioner fundholding scheme introduced in the United Kingdom in 1991. Under this scheme, groups of primary care physicians were allocated a budget with which to buy certain services for their patients and were allowed to use the savings for the benefit of patients. Fundholding attracted interest in a number of countries as a way of stimulating improvements in the use of resources. In the United Kingdom and other countries, attempts were made to ensure that 'money followed the patient' as a way of creating incentives for providers to be responsive to patients.

THE IMPACT OF REFORMS

What has been the impact of these reforms? This question is not easy to answer because comprehensive evaluations have rarely been conducted. It is also difficult to disentangle the effects of one set of policies from others, particularly given that most countries have used a cocktail of approaches. Indeed, although it is possible to separate and classify different policies for analytical purposes, in practice health care reforms were rarely packaged in such a logical fashion, and there was considerable overlap between the themes identified above. A further complication is that many of those who have evaluated health care reforms note the difficulty of reaching firm judgements at this stage, particularly when some of the initiatives that have been pursued have been implemented relatively recently and when a longer period of time is needed to assess their impact. Nevertheless, by piecing together evidence from a number of sources, it is possible to describe the direction that the reforms have taken and to draw on the results of different studies to distil some broad conclusions from experience so far. Of particular value in this respect are the studies carried out by the OECD and the WHO, as well as analyses produced by researchers who have examined specific aspects of the reform process.

To begin with, and to reiterate an earlier point, it is clear that policies to contain costs at the macro level have been effective in most systems. As Hurst noted in his study of health care reform in seven OECD countries, integrated models appear to be most successful in containing costs followed by contract models and reimbursement models.[12] This conclusion was qualified by Abel-Smith who, in a subsequent analysis of health care reform in a larger group of OECD countries, argued that political will was the key factor in accounting for cost containment. As he commented:

> a strong case can be made that the level of expenditure and success in cost containment simply depends on the strength of the determination of governments and the political power of the various actors who may attempt to resist controls. Governments which are united in the drive to control costs seem to be able to find ways to do so, whatever the system of organisation of the services.[13]

As we have noted a range of instruments were used to contain costs with the mixture varying between countries. Of particular significance were controls over the *supply* of services, such as fixed budgets for hospitals and policies to limit hospital building and the use of medical equipment. Much less important were measures to influence the *demand* for health care. Cost shifting to users was advocated by some as an instrument of reform but in practice it gained little support among policy makers. This reflected concerns at the impact of charges on access to health care and equity in service delivery. Public finance therefore continued to be the preferred method of health services funding and voluntary insurance was largely supplementary to public finance.

The impact of reforms designed to increase efficiency and enhance responsiveness to service users is less clear. As a number of studies have suggested, there appears to be increasing convergence in the content of these reforms. This includes a preference for the public contract model, the use of managed markets within this model, and the development of incentives for providers to improve performance. Following an analysis of the development of these reforms at an early stage in their evolution, Hurst concluded:

> the public contract model combines more desirable features than either the public reimbursement or the public integrated models.... Only the contract model is suited *both* to the pursuit of macro-economic efficiency *and* to the pursuit of micro-economic efficiency. In addition, the contract model seems better suited to self-regulation and appropriate provider autonomy than either of the other two models.[14]

The same study went further to suggest that the introduction of competition into publicly financed health care systems along the lines proposed in the United Kingdom, the Netherlands and Germany 'offer prospects for increased consumer choice, producer autonomy and efficiency in the health systems concerned, without sacrifices in overall cost control or equity'.[15]

It also noted, in a more cautious vein, that 'Managed markets within public health care systems are, however, still relatively untried' and that

> certain trade-offs cannot be escaped: between responsiveness and equity for example; and between cost-containment and choice. All we can hope for, is that by raising the productivity of health care systems, the reformed systems will ease the pain involved in such trade-offs.[16]

Yet if there is a large measure of consensus that the shift from the public integrated model to the public contract model is at the heart of recent reforms, there is less agreement with Hurst's judgement that this shift is likely to be beneficial. Both analysts and policy makers offer different interpretations of the evidence that is available and there is a continuing debate about the effect of markets in health care. In this debate, the emphasis has moved away from the simple dichotomy of 'planning versus markets' – if this ever existed – to a discussion of how the two may be combined. Put another way, there has been a search for a middle way between idealized centrally planned, command-and-control health systems and those in which market principles are favoured. This has been noted by Hsiao, among others, who has argued:

> Relying on the government to provide health services may not be a much better alternative than the market-based systems. Public-sector provision of health services often suffers from bureaucratic inefficiency, long waiting time, and unresponsive public sector workers protected by their unions.... National experiences teach us that neither pure centrally-planned nor free-market health systems can achieve maximum efficiency. A complex mixed system seems to be the answer.[17]

Hsiao's point has been underscored by Jonsson in his review of health care reforms in Sweden and other countries. As Jonsson concludes:

> All successful health care policies are piecemeal and there is no perfect health care system. The choice is not between an imperfect integrated system and a perfect market system, nor between an imperfect market system and a perfect integrated system. Both systems are imperfect. Thus, it is the optimal trade off between markets and hierarchies that gives the best value for money in the health care system.[18]

Jonsson's comment reflects increasing appreciation that reforms need to proceed in a pragmatic fashion with policy makers continually evaluating the impact of their interventions and adjusting their course accordingly. If market-oriented reforms are pursued, and this is not the case everywhere, the puzzle is how best to regulate the market to combine the anticipated benefits of competitive strategies with the need for effective planning and coordination. In this process, the challenge is to avoid the worst of all worlds, namely the risk that a continuing emphasis on inappropriate forms of regulation will blunt the impact of the market and will result in increasing fragmentation in service provision and additional transaction costs without commensurate gains in efficiency and responsiveness.

Experience of implementing the reforms in a number of systems suggests that it would be wrong to exaggerate the extent of convergence noted in early studies of recent reform efforts. While a number of common themes and trends can be identified, important differences remain. This was highlighted in a comparative analysis of health care reform in the Netherlands, Sweden and the United Kingdom which noted:

> Policy makers seeking to tackle weaknesses in the financing and delivery of health services are developing similar policy instruments in different countries and are using them to stimulate more efficiency in resource use and increased responsiveness to users.... Notwithstanding the similarities, important and interesting differences of approach emerge on deeper analysis.... The existence of these differences indicates that the degree of convergence in health care reform may not be as great as first appears. Put another way, although the vocabulary of reform may be international, terms such as 'managed market', 'budgetary incentives', 'purchasers', and 'providers' are interpreted differently in the three countries.[19]

It should also be noted that some countries have decided not to embark on major reforms at this stage and have concentrated instead on making marginal adjustments to existing systems.

The existence of different kinds of health care markets, or rather different sets of relationship between purchasers and providers, is illustrated in Figure 1.5.[20] Using the terms set out there, it can be suggested that the United Kingdom reforms have resulted in a shift from a monopolistic integrated model to a monopsonistic contract model. This is in contrast to the reforms taking place in the Netherlands where a competitive contract model is gradually replacing a system which was based on bilateral monopsonistic contracts and monopolistic provider reimbursement. Outside Europe developments in the United States are leading to the emergence of the competitive integrated model represented by health maintenance organizations (HMOs). The performance of HMOs appears to compare favourably with voluntary insurance and fee-for-service medicine and has led to increasing interest within Europe in this approach to health care financing and delivery.[21] Indeed, it has been argued that the competitive integrated model may combine the best features of the competitive contract model (as in the Netherlands) and the monopolistic contract model (as in the United Kingdom).[22] However, this is a hypothesis to be tested rather than a firm conclusion based on research evidence, and it should be viewed with caution in view of the cost and inequity of the United States health care system.

		Providers of care	
		Price competition	No price competition
Third–party payers	Price competition	1a Competitive reimbursement model 1b Competitive contract model 1c Competitive integrated model	3a Monopolistic provider reimbursement model 3b Monopolistic contract model
	No price competition	2a Competitive provider reimbursement model 2b Monopsonistic contract model	4a Non–competitive reimbursement model 4b Bilateral monopolistic contract model 4 Monopolistic integrated model

Figure 1.5 Different models of the relation between the third-party payers ('insurers') and the providers of health care
Source: van de Ven *et al.* (1994). Reproduced by permission of Elsevier Science.

What is clear is that within Europe the key difference between the United Kingdom and the Netherlands is that in the United Kingdom competition is mainly between providers whereas in the Netherlands the aim is to promote competition between insurers and providers. A similar objective is being pursued in Germany and Israel. The argument for competition between insurers is that this may provide insurers with an incentive to act as an effective agent on behalf of users, thereby offering greater choice. Such a model would in this way address one of the perceived weaknesses of integrated systems, namely lack of responsiveness to users. Competition between insurers may also create stronger incentives for efficiency by motivating insurers to reduce the cost of care in order to keep premiums down. Against this there is the danger of cream skimming and risk selection unless the insurance market is effectively regulated, and competing insurers also tend to increase administrative costs. Recognition of this danger led a major WHO review of health care reform to urge caution in the adoption of reforms designed to promote competition between insurers.[23] Instead, the review argued that effort should concentrate on reforms to the supply or delivery of health care as these had demonstrated greater success.

The key issue here, alluded to already, is that policies designed to increase efficiency, choice and responsiveness may make it difficult to achieve other objectives. In particular, access and equity may suffer. A further risk, noted by a number of analysts, is that market oriented reforms may increase transaction costs. It is also possible that success in cost containment at the macro level may be difficult to sustain as reforms designed to increase efficiency, choice and responsiveness put pressure on constrained budgets. The challenge for policy makers in this situation is to make trade-offs between different objectives.

Weale and colleagues have illustrated the nature of these trade-offs in Figure 1.6 which compares the United Kingdom and United States using four criteria.[24] As they note, improvements in performance in one direction may only be possible if achievements in another are sacrificed. The way in which these choices or trade-offs is resolved depends on the values of policy makers and the outcome will vary between countries. Furthermore, if important values such as equity appear to be threatened by health care reform, then policy makers may decide to modify the reforms to protect these values. And as Evans reminds us, in analysing health care reforms it is essential to look behind the rhetoric and examine the distributional effects of the policies that are pursued.[25] Changes to health care financing and delivery result in winners and losers and yet this is often not accounted for in the studies that are undertaken.

One of the issues that arises out of this is the extent to which policy makers are willing to be explicit about their values and objectives. As Pierson has shown in a study of welfare reform in the United States and the United Kingdom, politicians often resort to incremental changes in policy because of actual or potential opposition to radical and explicit changes in welfare programmes.[26] Over a period of time, these incremental changes may have a significant cumulative effect. The result has been to produce major savings or cuts in public spending and effectively to privatize aspects of welfare provision. An example which helps to illustrate this in the

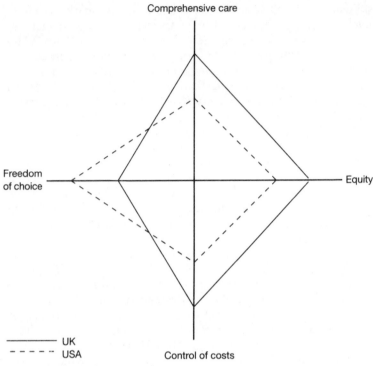

Figure 1.6   The trade-offs of health care financing
Source: Weale (1988)

United Kingdom is long-term care which has gradually moved from an NHS responsibility to become mainly a matter for local authorities or for private provision. This has happened as a consequence of a series of incremental decisions with the effect that the principle of comprehensive health service provision has been eroded. The implication for the health policy analyst is that the focus of study needs to be both major policy initiatives and routine decision making. To concentrate solely on the former may result in important changes being overlooked or underestimated.

   From this brief overview, it is clear that a number of lessons have emerged from recent experience. At the same time there is much that is not known and there is continuing debate about the interpretation of the evidence. All the more reason therefore to examine further the experience of countries at the forefront of reform to shed light on how the inevitable trade-offs in health policy are being handled. In this way, it should be possible to be clearer about the future direction that reform should take and the choices available to policy makers. What is already apparent is that there is no such thing as an ideal health care system and to advocate a single solution to the challenge of health financing and delivery is to ignore not only the emerging evidence but also the need to respect the traditions and cultures of different countries.

THE PLAN OF THE BOOK

In an attempt to fill some of the gaps in our knowledge, the chapters that follow offer up to date and expert analyses of experiences in five countries. In Chapter 2, Brad Kirkman-Liff provides an overview of health care reform in the United States. He traces the evolution of health services in the United States during this century and explains why the Clintons' reforms failed. Kirkman-Liff then reviews the legacy of the Clintons' plans and the way in which reform is proceeding even in the absence of federal legislation. In his conclusion, he reminds European readers of the weaknesses of the United States system and of the gains already made in those countries that have achieved universal population coverage.

Chapter 3 reviews the reforms introduced in the United Kingdom. The editor offers an interpretation of the origins of the reforms and their implementation drawing on a variety of published sources. The emerging balance sheet is evenly weighed. While there appear to have been some positive outcomes from the reforms, unanticipated problems have arisen in the process. This has led politicians to depart from the original design in a number of respects and a range of new policy initiatives have been pursued.

Chapter 4 examines experience in Sweden. Clas Rehnberg describes the range of reforms that have been pursued and examines the key role of the county councils in promoting change. The decentralized nature of the Swedish health care system has led to variations in the approach taken in different regions while at the same time enabling comparisons to be made between those county councils that have pursued reforms and those that have not. Rehnberg summarizes the evidence that is available about the impact of these reforms and highlights areas in which difficulties have arisen.

Chapter 5 focuses on the Netherlands. Wynand van de Ven explains the background to reforms in the Netherlands, the recommendations of the Dekker report and the way in which these recommendations have subsequently been amended. Although the Dutch reforms have not followed a smooth path of implementation, nevertheless some important changes have resulted. Van de Ven outlines policies recently announced by the government to guide the next stage of the reforms and looks forward to their likely impact.

In the final country chapter, Friedrich Wilhelm Schwartz and Reinhard Busse outline changes that have occurred in Germany. They emphasize the need to understand the historical and political context in which these reforms have been promulgated and the roles of different actors in the system. The importance of cost containment in Germany has led to a succession of reform laws and further changes are planned. This has provoked opposition from the interests most affected and threatens to undermine the consensus tradition of German politics.

The concluding chapter stands back from developments in individual countries to offer an overview of experience so far, focusing both on the process of reform and the results that have been achieved. In so doing, the chapter draws not only on the contributions to this book but also on other studies of health care reform. The aim in this chapter is to summarize what has been gleaned from experience so far as a guide for both practitioners and students of health policy.

NOTES

1 C.J. Ham, R. Robinson and M. Benzeval (1990) *Health Check*. London: King's Fund Institute; OECD (1992) *The Reform of Health Care: A Comparative Analysis of Seven OECD Countries*. Paris: Organisation for Economic Cooperation and Development; OECD (1994) *The Reform of Health Care Systems: A Review of Seventeen OECD Countries*. Paris: Organisation for Economic Cooperation and Development.

2 C.J. Ham, R. Robinson and M. Benzeval (1990) *Health Check*. London: King's Fund Institute.

3 OECD (1996) *OECD Health Data 96*. Paris: Organisation for Economic Cooperation and Development.

4 OECD (1995) *New Directions in Health Care Policy*. Paris: Organisation for Economic Cooperation and Development.

5 R.J. Maxwell (1988) Financing health care: lessons from abroad, *British Medical Journal*, 296: 1423–6.

6 OECD (1992) *The Reform of Health Care: A Comparative Analysis of*

Seven OECD Countries. Paris: Organisation for Economic Cooperation and Development; OECD (1994) *The Reform of Health Care Systems: A Review of Seventeen OECD Countries.* Paris: Organisation for Economic Cooperation and Development.

7 OECD (1992) *The Reform of Health Care: A Comparative Analysis of Seven OECD Countries.* Paris: Organisation for Economic Cooperation and Development.

8 OECD (1992) *The Reform of Health Care: A Comparative Analysis of Seven OECD Countries.* Paris: Organisation for Economic Cooperation and Development.

9 OECD (1995) *New Directions in Health Care Policy.* Paris: Organisation for Economic Cooperation and Development; C.J. Ham, R. Robinson and M. Benzeval (1990) *Health Check.* London: King's Fund Institute.

10 W. Dekker (1987) *Willingness to Change.* The Hague: SDU.

11 R. Griffiths (1983) *NHS Management Inquiry.* London: DHSS.

12 OECD (1992) *The Reform of Health Care: A Comparative Analysis of Seven OECD Countries.* Paris: Organisation for Economic Cooperation and Development.

13 OECD (1994) *The Reform of Health Care Systems: A Review of Seventeen OECD Countries.* Paris: Organisation for Economic Cooperation and Development, p. 40.

14 OECD (1992) *The Reform of Health Care: A Comparative Analysis of Seven OECD Countries.* Paris: Organisation for Economic Cooperation and Development, p. 149.

15 OECD (1992) *The Reform of Health Care: A Comparative Analysis of Seven OECD Countries.* Paris: Organisation for Economic Cooperation and Development, p. 144.

16 OECD (1992) *The Reform of Health Care : A Comparative Analysis of Seven OECD Countries.* Paris: Organisation for Economic Cooperation and Development, p. 151.

17 W.C. Hsiao (1994) 'Marketization' – the illusory magic pill. *Health Economics,* 3: 356. See also R. Saltman and C. von Otter (1992) *Planned Markets and Public Competition: Strategic Reform in Northern European Health Systems.* Buckingham: Open University Press.

18 B. Jonsson (1996) Making sense of health care reform, in OECD (ed.) *Health Care Reform. The Will to Change.* Paris: Organisation for Economic Cooperation and Development.

19 C.J. Ham and M. Brommels (1994) Health care reform in the Netherlands, Sweden and the United Kingdom. *Health Affairs,* 13 (4): p. 107.

20 W.P.M.M. van de Ven, F.T. Schut and F.F.H. Rutten (1994) Forming and reforming the market for third-party purchasing of health care. *Social Science and Medicine,* 39 (10): 1405–12.

21 H.S. Luft (1994) Health maintenance organisations: Is the United States experience applicable to ourselves? in OECD (ed.) *Health:*

Quality and Choice. Paris: Organisation for Economic Cooperation and Development.

22 W.P.M.M. van de Ven, F.T. Schut and F.F.H. Rutten (1994) Forming and reforming the market for third-party purchasing of health care. *Social Science and Medicine*, 39 (10): 1405–12.

23 WHO (1996) *European Health Care Reforms, Analysis of Current Strategies*. Copenhagen: World Health Organization.

24 A. Weale (ed.) (1988) *Cost and Choice in Health Care:* London: King's Fund.

25 R.G. Evans (1996) Marketing markets, regulating regulators: Who gains? Who loses? What hopes? What scope? in OECD (ed.) *Health Care Reform. The Will to Change*. Paris: Organisation for Economic Cooperation and Development.

26 P. Pierson (1994) *Dismantling the Welfare State?* Cambridge: Cambridge University Press.

2

THE UNITED STATES
Bradford Kirkman-Liff

INTRODUCTION

Politically-determined, government-directed structural health care reform is unlikely to happen in the US for the next 25 years. There are two major impediments to health reform in America. The first is the history of incremental health reform for the last 85 years and the past failures at structural reform. The second is the continuing decline of faith in government and politics as a mechanism to address social problems. In this chapter I will review those two impediments, the current trends in the US health system that are giving us many of the disadvantages of reform with few of the benefits (some call this 'reform without reform'), and will conclude with a few tentative lessons for Europeans from the American experience.

THE FAILURE OF REFORM EFFORTS

Structural health care reform in the US has been a story of ever-slowing progress. Each effort over the past 85 years to reform the structure of health care in a systematic, comprehensive manner has only resulted in incremental reforms that retard and prevent fundamental reform and increase the rigidity of an inefficient and inequitable system. To understand the failures of the past 85 years in health reform requires an appreciation of the American system of government, intentionally designed to be internally conflicting.

The US is not a unitary, parliamentary, party democracy. The nation is split into 50 states and one federal government. Domestic issues such as health care are intertwined with the issue of state versus federal authority and power. Further complications are the ethnic and cultural diversity of the US and the variation in state economies and state-level welfare and tax policies.

In the US there are separately elected executive and legislative branches, and the legislative bodies are themselves split. We have to independently elect 102 legislative bodies and 51 executives. Our system is not based on parties; each politician is independently elected, and has to conduct his or her own fundraising and campaigning. Political action committees are essential mechanisms to raising the $5,000,000 needed for a Senate race and the $25,000,000 for a Presidential race. Party discipline is very weak, and the influence of lobbying groups is very strong. The US is not a full democracy, but a republic; less than half of the eligible population votes, and so it only requires about 30 per cent of the total population to have effective control of the federal and state governments.

Under this structure any amount of controversy or a lack of wide political support for a domestic issue means the end of any reform proposal. The conventional wisdom in American health care reform circles is that the failure of the Clinton proposal proves again that incremental reform is the only way to move forward in domestic policy. The debate in the US about structural reform has arisen eight times, but each effort has produced either incremental reform that made the next effort at reform more difficult, or no reform at all. The following brief review of the previous efforts draws on the work of Starr, Stevens and others.[1]

Act I. The 1910s: A partial vision of structural reform

In the 1910s the US was already decades behind much of the industrial world in establishing a system of health coverage for all members of society. Germany had 25 years of experience with their compulsory insurance system, enacted in 1883. The US system at that time was highly tiered. The top tier consisted of solo practice physicians and not-for-profit private hospitals serving the upper income group who generally paid out of pocket. The bottom tier consisted of public hospitals and public health clinics, staffed by medical students, serving the poor. One middle tier was the uninsured middle class, who did not want to use the public hospitals but faced financial difficulty when it tried to access the top tier. The other middle tier was the growing insured middle class, who either had private insurance or were covered by employer-sponsored health programmes.

A number of reform advocates proposed that the US adopt a German-style compulsory insurance system. These proposals were attacked by the physicians, hospitals, pharmaceutical firms, industrial manufacturers, and the growing private health insurance industry. Each perceived that the threat to loss of autonomy or profits by compulsory insurance was greater than any potential benefits from increased coverage. The labour movement generally did not support compulsory insurance as it argued that bargaining for health benefits would gain new members for the union movement. In many ways the health care trade associations echoed their positions of 85 years ago during the Clinton reform debate.

Act II. The 1930s: A compromise model

A number of physicians, economists, and public health advocates organized the Committee on Costs of Medical Care in 1926, which obtained support from eight private foundations and conducted a five year research programme. Their research found an inefficiently organized system with severe barriers to care. They recommended a number of comprehensive reforms, including the formation of prepaid group practices financed initially by voluntary insurance and government payment of premiums for the poor. These prepaid groups would receive membership dues and would employ physicians on salaries to care for their defined membership. The committee did not endorse either national health insurance or a German-style compulsory workplace model at that time.

Nonetheless, these proposals were attacked by the physicians, hospitals, manufacturers and private health insurance industry. These groups again contended that there was no need for increased government involvement in health care for the middle class or the poor, and that prepaid group practice was a short step away from socialized medicine. They argued that the poor were adequately served by the public programmes, and the market could create insurance products that the middle class could purchase. The middle class supported the concept that their access to health care could best be served by linking their care to the upper middle class, private insurance and solo fee-for-service practice, not by linking their health care to the poor, public provision or group practice.[2] The controversy over the Committee on Costs of Medical Care – despite its middle-of-the-road position – convinced a number of Democrats to exclude national health insurance as a component to the Social Security Act.

Private, not-for-profit insurance with voluntary enrolment was able to meet the needs of the middle class through community rating. These insurers – Blue Cross and Blue Shield plans – charged uniform rates to all members. There was an internal cross-subsidization from the young and healthy to the old and sick, and from large businesses to small businesses. The participants generally felt that subsidies through a community rating structure were preferable to a government-run, tax-financed system. The success of that incremental reform created the pattern that has been followed time after time. Rather than create a unitary system, each debate on structural health reform ends up incrementally adjusting the tiered system, further dividing patients, institutions, providers, and payers.

Act III. World War II: The wage freeze loophole

The four tier structure was aided by the labour unions and large corporations during the war. Unions continued to prefer to bargain with employers for health benefits, and feared that a national health insurance programme would deprive them of one of the benefits that attracted employees to unions. Employers were more willing to provide a discrete benefit to their own employees than pay generic taxes for a benefit for all citizens.

These two motivations came together during the war when a wage and price freeze was in effect. General Motors, Ford and the United Auto Workers met with White House officials to obtain a ruling on the provision of health benefits to workers. Would the employer's contribution be seen as taxable income? The answer was no. Would the benefit be seen as an increase in wages? The answer was no. Those war time decisions put in place a mechanism of a tax subsidy for employer-provided health benefits.

The employer was neutral between paying higher wages and higher benefits, but the employee gained by not paying taxes on the value of the benefits. Suddenly the working middle class had broad health coverage. And an incremental reform – tax-subsidization – created another impediment to unitary reform. While concerns were raised at this time that stimulating the provision of insurance through this mechanism would only delay structural reform, the need to provide coverage quickly overwhelmed those concerns.

Act IV. The late 1940s: A gesture

After the end of the war President Truman revisited the idea of a unitary national health insurance programme. As in the 1930s it was attacked by the same parties: physicians, hospitals, business and private health insurers. They argued that socialized medicine (even though Truman only proposed socialized insurance, with provision left in the private sector) would lower quality and access. The poor were adequately served by the public hospitals and teaching clinics, and the rest of the country was served by the private system.

Truman's proposal died in Congress without ever coming to a vote. The debate saw the largest public relations effort ever mounted in the US by an organization: the American Medical Association (AMA) raised more than $1,000,000 to defeat the Truman proposals. The tactic of the AMA to constantly label the Truman proposal as 'government-controlled socialized medicine' was again echoed in attacks on the Clinton proposal, even though both retained fee-for-service payment, private physician practice and non-profit hospitals.

Act V. The early 1960s: The grand incremental reform

The return of Democrats to the White House led some to think that a structural health reform proposal would be brought forward. The debate over reform did not return to the Roosevelt and Truman proposals for either national health insurance or compulsory work-place insurance, but rather meeting the needs of a specific group: the elderly. It was acknowledged that the earlier reforms of private insurance and tax-subsidization for employer contributions had not addressed the elderly. Medicare and Medicaid were seen as incremental reforms that preserved the rest of the health care system. As they were intended to be compatible with the voluntary insurance model, both programmes were based on fee-for-service payment. It was felt that by covering the poor with Medicaid, the elderly through Medicare, and working Americans and their children through employer-provided, tax-subsidized private insurance, America would have universal coverage.

The two programmes are organized very differently and have enjoyed varying political favour. Medicare is a nationally uniform programme, with standardized eligibility, benefits and payments, administered by private insurers under contract to the federal government. Medicaid varies state by state, with different eligibility, benefits and payments, administered by each state independently. Medicare is seen as an earned entitlement that the elderly have paid for with their social security taxes; Medicaid is seen as a part of welfare charity given to the poor (who are frequently seen as undeserving).

Medicare and Medicaid as incremental reforms created new constituencies that wanted to protect those programmes. The elderly, in the 30 years since Medicare, have become very attached to their indemnity coverage with direct access to specialists. Any proposal to reform Medicare comes under attack. The elderly also are wary of proposals for global structural reform; they are afraid that their programme will be lost. Medicaid also has its advocates. A number of institutions – community health centres, inner-city public hospitals, and medical schools – have learned how to earn adequate profits from Medicaid payments. Unitary reform would threaten their exclusive coverage of the low income groups.

Act VI. The early 1970s: A near compromise

Within six years of the enactment of Medicare and Medicaid it became very clear to all politicians that their incremental reforms had been poorly designed. Unfortunately, the Democratic and Republican views on the types of structural reforms that were needed were opposed. Democrats wanted expansion of access to care through universal fee-for-service insurance, while Republicans wanted to control costs by replacing the incentives of fee-for-service payment with managed systems of care.

The Democrats who had supported Medicare realized very quickly that universal coverage had not been achieved. Too many employers – despite the tax subsidy – did not offer their employees (especially hourly employees) health benefits. The 50 states were not uniform in cooperating in Medicaid; many set their eligibility levels so low that only 25 per cent of the poor were covered. The Democrats under Senator Kennedy introduced a national health insurance proposal. It called for a single unitary system to fold those with employer-based or Medicaid coverage into Medicare.

The Republicans saw a different problem. The design of Medicare, Medicaid and employment-linked coverage all resulted in rapid cost increases, due to the inherent incentives in fee-for-service payment. They sought reform that would lower costs for the government. Large corporations were also experiencing rapid increases in health benefit costs, and sought similar solutions. President Nixon, a Californian, looked home and found prepaid group practices such as Kaiser-Permanente. These integrated systems of care had been a focus of the Committee on Costs of Medical Care. The expansion of prepaid group practice, or health maintenance organizations (HMOs), was seen as an incremental reform that would control costs, without government control of the health system. In a sense, HMOs would be for-profit cost regulators.

After months of debate it seemed that the Democrats could embrace cost-controls and HMOs and replace a unitary insurance system with a German-style compulsory workplace model, if the Republicans would add compulsory insurance to their HMO concept. It is unclear if a compromise could have been reached. A number of parties (especially physicians) feared that such a compromise would give them the worst of all possible worlds: lower incomes, lower professional autonomy, and the inability to select their patients. Yet the adoption of the need for structural health reform by the conservatives created an opportunity. The window closed with the Watergate break-in and eventual resignation of President Nixon. In retrospect, 1974 may have been the last opportunity for political agreement on structural reform.

Act VII. The late 1970s through the early 1990s: The Carter-Reagan-Bush health policy nap

The election of President Carter seemed to indicate that progress on health reform would happen, given the preliminary steps taken in the early 1970s that had been pointing to a compromise of compulsory private HMO coverage. Such was not the case. The costs of Medicare and Medicaid were mounting, and there was only consensus for incremental cost regulation. A vigorous attack on government regulation of hospital costs was launched by the hospital industry, aided by the physicians and insurers (who saw that they might be regulated next). A nationwide uniform cost containment strategy failed; instead, hospitals promised a voluntary effort to control costs which failed after three years to meet its targets.

The election of President Reagan indicated a new period in the health reform debate. Health reform was not addressed by the Republicans prior to election, except for platitudes that free-market competition and deregulation would lower costs and therefore make insurance affordable. The 1980s saw continued growth of HMOs as employers tried to control their own costs. States narrowed eligibility for Medicaid, and Medicare reduced provider payments and introduced per-admission payments (diagnosis related groups) for hospital care and a new fee schedule system for physicians (resource-based relative value scale). A number of states ended Certificate-of-Need regulations on hospital construction, triggering a building boom of excess capacity. The decade ended with the highest rates of health care inflation.[3]

The greatest impact on the health system in the 1980s was the movement of large corporations to self-insurance. Businesses wanted to lower their costs for employee health benefits. Some employers made major efforts to reduce their benefits which triggered a number of strikes. As benefits could not be significantly reduced, they sought to reduce their costs, and self-insurance became the solution. Rather than paying premiums to health insurers, employers simply informed their employees that as a benefit they would have their medical bills paid, subject to deductibles and co-payments. The employers retained the financial risk, but also retained all of the cash, and cut out the marketing and profits of the insurers. Self-insurance also exempted the employer from all state regulation of health insurance. Employers can retroactively change the benefits under self-insurance.

The biggest impact of self-insurance in the 1980s was that it broke the unstated compact that was behind the decisions in the 1930s and 1940s to have a private, not-for-profit, voluntary health insurance system. It ended community rating and moved to group experience rating. Each employer would pay unique rates, based on the age, gender, and health experience of its employees, if it continued to buy insurance. As small employers (those with less than 250 employees) could not self-insure because their actuarial risks are higher due to their small size, they were left with purchasing insurance that often was double the costs experienced by large employers. Many firms below 20 employees were priced out of the market, and many other firms no longer provided health benefits to non-managerial employees. Combined with Medicaid cutbacks, the number of uninsured grew. The early 1990s saw an upsurge in activity about health care reform, but the conventional wisdom was correct; nothing would even be attempted until after the 1992 election.[4] The failure of the Pepper Commission to reach a broad consensus among its members on comprehensive reform indicated that an attempt at structural reform was a few years away.[5]

Before the curtain rises on Act VIII, I want to summarize the delivery and insurance structure that is the target of structural reforms. Private, voluntary insurance created in the 1910s and reinforced by incremental reforms and government subsidies in the past 80 years has locked into place a number of problems:

Fee-for-service payment

It is ingrained in American health care providers and institutions that a higher volume is rewarded by higher income. Fee-for-service payment is the norm; capitation payments or budgets are seen as alien concepts. Even in the areas with the highest proportion of the population enrolled in HMOs, physicians and hospitals still refer to fee-for-service equivalents or per day rates and go through elaborate calculation to convert population-based capitation payments to those norms.

Technological infatuation

American patients and physicians love technology. The use of a computer in a diagnostic or therapeutic instrument reassures all parties that the most up-to-date and sophisticated equipment is in use. The fee-for-service model encourages the continual adoption of new technology, because the highest fees are those for the newest technology.[6]

Specialization

The fee-for-service model combined with technology leads to an overspecialization of American physicians. The incentive is scientific and economic. Fees are highest when services are unique, and technology provides the opportunity for increasing uniqueness of services and intellectual challenges. Medical schools view themselves as centres of scientific research, and recruit those students who have the highest promise for intellectually challenging work. The physicians in the US tend to specialize and subspecialize out of scientific curiosity, economic rewards, and simply boredom with primary care.

Acute intervention

The fee-for-service mentality and overspecialization lead to a focus on acute medical interventions, especially surgery, and little attention to long-term care, rehabilitation, or prevention. This has shaped our entire hospital and ambulatory care infrastructure.

Primary care neglect

The concept of a primary care physician is alien to the US.[7] Most Americans believe that the natural order is direct access to specialists. Despite 50 years of HMOs in California and other western states, the primary care gatekeeping physician is still not widely accepted. The medical community does not accept the idea of a primary care gatekeeper; many specialists feel that family medicine physicians in HMOs underrefer patients.

Separation of payer and provider accountability and responsibility

The model of insurance and financing as distinct from health care provision is inherent in the US structure. Every insurance programme repeatedly reminds its beneficiaries that the insurer does not make medical care decisions. They adjudicate claims, not the medical judgements of the providers. Managed care plans argue that they do not restrict access or ration care when they state they will not pay the provider for the care. The patient is still free to request or demand the care, and it is the provider who is refusing the treatment, not the insurer. In this model providers are expected to provide whatever care they feel that the patient needs, and they should not be swayed by an insurer's prospective decision to deny payment for that service.

Diversity and complexity

The incremental approach of tax-subsidized employment-based insurance, Medicare, and Medicaid has led to great diversity of insurance mechanisms, with profit the motivation for most insurers. Rules and regulations differ insurer by insurer, state by state, year to year, and, in the case of self-insured employers, day to day.

Discrimination and risk avoidance

The system of diverse, private for-profit insurance competitors, government programmes for the elderly and the poor, self-insurance by large employers, and voluntary choice on the provision and purchase of insurance has led to a market driven by risk selection and risk avoidance. The simplest way to make money in the US health insurance market for most of the last 80 years was to avoid high risk persons, families, businesses, industries and communities.

The focus has been on selling policies to those who will have limited use of health care services, and not covering or limiting coverage for those with risk of substantial use. The movement in the last 10 years from community rating to experience rating has continued the trend. All insurers worry about underpricing their experience rated products, and through denials of coverage or pre-existing condition limitations try to avoid risk. Yet reform was more about changing these structural elements. Values and politics were what doomed health care reform, three values associated with the voluntary insurance system that underlaid the reform debates, and three groups very worried about politics.

First, health insurance and health coverage has never been seen as a right or a societal obligation in the US but simply as a voluntary purchase by a consumer. Uwe Reinhardt refers to the newest advocates of this position as the 'food people', in that they view health care as no different from food.[8] The 'food people' argue that in the US we do not get together and pool our money and eat collectively; we purchase our own meals with our own money and eat our own food. The government has a very limited role in food: assuring that truly impoverished persons do not starve to death, some assurance that food meets minimal wholesomeness standards, and some price stabilization for politically powerful farmers. Food is more essential to life than health care, and so why shouldn't health care be treated the same way?

Applied to health care and health insurance, the 'food people' argue that individuals should buy their own coverage and purchase their own care on a fee-for-service basis. In their view, group insurance and pooling of risks across persons of different health status, age or income is flawed. They view insurance as similar to compulsory company cafeterias. These advocates attack the idea of employer-sponsored coverage. A number of their reform proposals called for reduction in the tax incentives for group insurance and a reduction in coverage. They often propose a new tax subsidy for individual savings accounts for medical expenses. They also view Medicare as a flawed model, and would prefer that social security simply gave to each person a fixed voucher for the purchase of individual insurance. Medicaid should only apply to the truly destitute in life-threatening emergencies. Charity hospitals and teaching programmes who want to serve the uninsured can do so in order to fulfil their mission.

Second, and related to the ideas of the 'food people', is the view held by a number of health economists that health insurance –

especially group health insurance – is a flawed concept. They have two fears. The first is moral hazard; as insurance stimulates increased demand, it is inherently inefficient. The second is cross-subsidization; group coverage means that the old and sick pay the same as the young and healthy, and this is inherently inefficient. To them, health insurance should only be about protecting individual assets, purchased on an individual basis.[9] Insurance should not enable someone to obtain care that they could not obtain without insurance. Under this model, all insurance should have high deductibles and co-payments.[10] Concepts such as equity, dignity, solidarity, and social justice are generally missing from their vocabulary.

Third, there is very broad acceptance among the insured and non-poor that inequity for the poor and uninsured and a highly tiered system is legitimate. The concept of income, wealth and position allowing one to purchase better health care for oneself and one's family is seen as a fundamental value. Many in the US accept rationing by price for those who have low and moderate income and rationing by medical decisions for those who are mandated to be in or choose managed care, but they do not accept rationing for themselves in their own health care. Many in the US do not want to be in managed care for themselves, or at least want extensive out-of-plan benefits. Individual tax-advantaged savings accounts (called Medical Savings Accounts) will be seen as serving those who are in point-of-service choice managed care plans and those who purchase catastrophic indemnity coverage. The ideology of the 'food people', the logic of the 'moral hazard' health economists, and the wide acceptance of a tiered system combined to justify to three important groups that structural health reform was not just unnecessary but a bad idea: politicians, corporations, and a majority of the electorate.

Structural health care reform involves issues which politicians view as 'lose–lose' issues; no matter how they vote on a proposal, a sizeable number of their constituents will be angry. Health care reform involves issues of abortion and family planning, taxation, redistribution of income, state versus federal political authority, regulation versus markets, and limitations of professional and corporate autonomy and profits. They simply prefer to let the market solve whatever problems there are in the health care system. At the same time, Medicare and Medicaid have created for politicians a growing budgetary problem. For more than 20 years it is the cost of existing programmes, not the unmet health care needs of the uninsured, that have preoccupied Congress.[11] There are also some politicians who do not want to reduce America's health care costs. They argue that controlling health care costs reduces the health care revenues and profits of those pharmaceutical companies, health insurers, for-profit hospital chains, and physicians who are major contributors to political campaigns.

Health care now represents 14 per cent of the US gross domestic product. That means that between 1 and 2 per cent of the entire US economy is composed of the profits from health insurance and medical care organizations. Most parties are making profits: health insurers, HMOs, hospitals, pharmaceutical companies, supply manufacturers and distributors, physicians, lawyers, public relations and marketing consultants and information systems vendors. With all of those people making so much money from the current system there is a large segment of the society that wants to avoid cost containment. While meeting the needs of the uninsured is an important issue to many of these organizations, they usually put their profitability ahead of these needs. A related issue is success with cost containment. Many large companies take the view that they have solved their health care problem, through self-insurance and aggressive use of HMOs. While structural reform could provide them with further benefits, many argue that their health care costs are now under control.

It is important to remember that voting participation is at the lowest level that it has been in the last 75 years, resulting in the voting electorate being highly skewed from the general population. The people who tend to vote are far more educated, wealthier, white, older, and insured than the overall US population. A solid majority of the *voting* public in the US has good health insurance coverage, receives high quality care, pays relatively little out of their own pocket for care, and fear that change will reduce their current benefits. As with politicians and corporations, the electorate is more concerned with maintaining their health care privileges than expanding access to the uninsured or controlling the overall system costs (although they do express concern over those issues).[12] While health care is not seen in as pejorative a light as welfare, there are still substantial variations in support along income, education and ethnicity lines.[13]

Act VIII. 1993–95: The Clintons

During the 1992 election campaign and afterwards there mistakenly appeared to be substantial support for structural reform of the system.[14] The Clintons felt that they could meet the Republican agenda of cost-containment and the Democratic agenda of universal coverage by returning to the near-compromise of 20 years ago: German-style compulsory workplace insurance, with financing and care integrated in managed care plans that would compete for members.[15] Many of their ideas harkened even further back – to the Committee on Costs of Medical Care from the 1930s. The Clintons added private, non-profit regional health purchasing alliances to contract with insurers (both indemnity and HMOs) using community rating, while allowing experience rating for those outside the purchasing alliances. Many of the components of the Clinton model were similar to those of Republican models, especially in the use of managed care and market competition.[16] The Clinton proposal did not create a British- or Scandinavian-style national health service; it did not create a Canadian- or French-style national health insurance system, it retained for-profit hospitals, health insurers, HMOs, and physician practices, and it called for market competition among plans to reduce costs.

The Clinton proposal as submitted to Congress was a complex system because it combined choice, private financing, private delivery, managed care, competition, universal coverage, and cost containment. It was the level of detail in the Clinton proposals that was partly to blame for what killed the proposals and at the same time was ignored by the most vocal opposition. This may seem contradictory, but that is not the case. The complexity of the details turned away those moderates in the electorate who had some interest in structural reform and who could have supported a simpler proposal. The focus on managed care was a threat to those with indemnity insurance. It was their fear of employer-imposed managed care that motivated a portion of the middle class's interest in structural reform as a way to keep indemnity coverage. The business community who believed it had solved its own health care cost problem turned against the Clinton proposal. They felt that some of the cost savings they had achieved by managed care would be used to subsidize the coverage for the previously uninsured.[17] The conservatives who opposed any reform – no matter how much it compromised the previous positions of the Republicans – simply labelled the Clinton model 'socialized medicine', the same tactic used 80 years ago. The support that appeared to be strong melted in the heat of debate.

Some have said that the President could have succeeded if he had simply announced his proposal in a document no longer than five pages, two weeks after his inauguration, rather than have a White House Task Force spend a year developing a document in excess of 1,000 pages. If the proposal had been sent to Congress in February 1993, it would have been the job of both parties in Congress to spend the next 18 months drafting the thousands of pages of legislation and regulations and reaching the difficult compromises.[18] But even if the Clintons had been excellent tacticians with health reform, it most likely would have failed, due to the second impediment: the decline of faith in government and politics in America.

THE DECLINE OF FAITH IN GOVERNMENT AND POLITICS

The last 30 years have seen an ever-worsening attitude in the US toward government and politics. The federal government is seen as the enemy of prosperity and freedom. Domestic terrorism such as the bombing in Oklahoma City in 1995 is not the aberration of a few individuals. There are tens of thousands of Americans who are preparing to take arms against the government, and hundreds of thousands of intellectual supporters, and millions who have an automatic response of hostility to any government official, programme or advocate.

This decline of faith in government and politics has several roots. I feel that one is the current structure of money politics in the US. Since the 1970s Political Action Committees (PACs) have become an essential feature of the political landscape. PACs are organizations which raise money from individuals and give it bundled to politicians for campaign expenses. The entire system is regulated and open: every contribution by an individual to a PAC is a matter of public record, as is every contribution from a PAC to a politician.[19] The process has institutionalized the role of money in politics. Many elected officials spend half of their time on fundraising, often by meeting with PAC representatives. Constant reporting as to which politicians are receiving money from which PAC has led the public to resign itself to money politics.[20]

The PAC system is so entrenched that one of the most difficult pieces of legislation to pass now is campaign financing reform legislation. Every lobbying organization knows that its success is tied to the current system. The PAC structure also forces an organization to decide on its highest priority issues: one analysis of the American Medical Association PAC contributions reveals that there was contradiction between whom the AMA gave money and the AMA's official position on three public health issues.[21] The PAC structure adds to the barriers of structural reform: the only way a politician can avoid offending his or her PAC contributors is to engage in the smallest incremental reforms.[22]

A second issue is the organization of lobbying and its ties to PACs. It is estimated that there are more than 500 health care related lobbying organizations in Washington, with five lobbyists for every elected official. Every one of those groups organizes visits by their members to legislators or their aides. It is often stated that the amount of time that one can spend with an elected official or their aide is a function of the amount of past PAC contributions: $100 gets 15 minutes with an aide, $6,000 gets 30 minutes with a Senator. Every lobbying group has glossy policy proposals with carefully reasoned arguments as to why their position is correct and the other 499 are wrong.[23] While coalitions do form, the internal wrangling results in an ever-increasing focus on turf issues and complex compromises. The Clintons tried to work through those details prior to introducing legislation, ended up with the 1,400 page bill, and all 500 groups started all over in Congress. It is often said that no one should ever watch sausage or legislation being made – but at least inside an abattoir the knives are visible.

A third issue involves the increased intensity of partisan politics and the public's disenchantment with partisan politics. A system of 102 legislative bodies and 51 executives would imply that leadership of all parties must work together, and for most of the twentieth century there was collaboration on a number of foreign and serious domestic issues. In the last several years the traditional agreements have become frayed, and the process of governing has slowed. Few issues are debated on their merits. Most proposals are introduced for the purpose of placing the other party in an embarrassing position.[24] Politicians are seen as continually running for re-election. Imagine if the parliamentary system in Britain was changed to one where the only activity is Question Time, the parliamentary majority vetoes the Prime Minister's cabinet appointments, the top four tiers of officials in all ministries are political appointments, and all members of the government – the Prime Minister, Cabinet Ministers, the opposition, and appointed officials and the entire civil service – are despised and ridiculed at every opportunity on radio and television. Is it surprising that most Americans have little faith in government or politics?

A fourth factor – and possibly the most important – is a growing unwillingness of Americans to address complexity and a belief that complexity is itself a sign of incompetence. Americans do not like complex, long-term solutions that affect themselves in a negative manner. They want quick fixes that impose their burden on someone else. Government is generally seen as proposing long-term, expensive, complex solutions. Every government programme is therefore seen as inherently wrong.

Not only do the public view politicians and government as incapable of governing, there is an increased sense that they shouldn't even try to govern. As structural reform of health care would not be quick or easy, and it would impose burdens on a large segment of the society that benefits from the current structure, structural reform is an inherently bad idea, and the Clintons' proposal proved the inability of government and politics to solve problems. The electorate is unwilling to confront and debate issues in any other terms than their own narrow interests and a belief that the right answer has to be quick, easy and not burdensome.[25]

The last factor applies specifically to health care. Americans are very defensive about the problems of the health care system. 'The health care system in America is the best in the world' ... is the slogan of Richard Scott, the CEO of Columbia/HCA, in his television advertisements, championing his company. Some have argued that there is nothing that we can learn from other countries and the problems in the US do not require structural reform: we should be teaching them how to dismantle socialized health care and introduce free markets.[26] Writers such as Fuchs and others have amply demonstrated that this contention is false.[27]

What killed the Clintons' reforms was both the past history of incremental reforms that created a powerful network of groups interested in preserving the current system and a decline in faith of the public on the ability of government to successfully provide sound structural reform. So we are faced with an inherent contradiction. The US health system needs fundamental, comprehensive structural reform if it is to achieve universal coverage and cost-containment. However, only incremental piecemeal reform is politically and economically feasible, and incremental piecemeal reform will only make the systems increasingly difficult to reform and increasingly complex.

The conclusion is that the US will never have structural health system reform. Costs will continue to rise, and access to care will continue to decline for a large minority of the electorate (a majority of the population). The US is likely to have a three tier system (or possibly more tiers) for the foreseeable future.[28] Health care reform in the United States in this century has been like someone trying to walk through hardening cement; each step takes one closer to a desired destination, but each step is more and more difficult, until movement ceases, far from the goal. Or maybe the US system is like an old computer programme; each revision adds more and more complexity to the system, and subroutines are added to correct errors in other subroutines, until the code is so gnarly that it can't be debugged. In either case, structural reform of the US health care system is probably off the political agenda for the next 25 years. This rather pessimistic view is unfortunately shared by others.[29]

REFORM WITHOUT REFORM

The US health system is not static: elements of the proposed Nixon–Clinton reforms are being implemented, but not systematically, and in ways that create new problems and exacerbate old ones. An especially ironic aspect is that many of the fears used by some of the opponents of the Clinton proposals to motivate opposition are now becoming real by the actions of some of the other opponents of the Clinton proposals. These 'reforms without reform' can be placed in three categories: market-driven structural change, state experiments with Medicaid and other programmes for the uninsured, and payer–provider initiatives in response to those structural changes and government experiments.

Structural change

The tiered structure of American health care is shifting, with more and more Americans moving into the lower tiers. The bottom tier is composed of the uninsured population with access limited to university and public hospital clinic and emergency rooms, who do not live in communities with voluntary managed care programmes for the uninsured. The number of uninsured is increasing and the length of time of being uninsured is increasing.

The second tier consists of persons with a minimal benefit package, often called a 'bare bones' package in the US. In this group are the Medicaid population mandated to enrol in managed care programmes, the employees of small employers whose only option is to enrol in bare bones managed care programmes with limited benefits, and those uninsured who live in communities with medical schools and/or public health departments which have created quasi-HMOs for the uninsured. This last type of programme involves the assignment of uninsured patients on a voluntary basis to clinics which serve as primary care gatekeepers for the uninsured. This strategy can reduce the costs usually absorbed by medical schools and public health departments whose emergency rooms are the default source of care for the uninsured.

The third tier is the largest, and is composed of the employed population, their dependants, and the Medicare population. All of these groups will have strong economic incentives to enrol in managed care plans. They will have the option of enrolling in point-of-service choice models or preferred provider plans, but those plans will be only slightly less restrictive than HMOs. They may also have the option of going into the top tier. However, the number of choices being offered to the members of this tier are decreasing. Employers are also increasingly requiring employees to pay the entire difference between the lowest cost managed care plan and the other plans. This forced choice by differential employee co-premiums was one item attacked by the Clinton opponents. The irony is that the Clinton model pooled the entire community so as to make the indemnity package affordable. In the current fragmented world of experience-rated employer-specific plans, indemnity coverage can cost the employee 10 times the monthly co-premium of an HMO. In the western US a number of employers are now only offering their employees a choice among managed care plans – far less choice than Clinton proposed.

The top tier is a fee-for-service segment outside managed care, with catastrophic indemnity coverage and tax-free savings accounts to pay for deductibles and co-insurance.

State experiments

A number of states acted before the Clinton proposals to expand coverage through Medicaid or other programmes.[30] Other states are enacting new experimental programmes since the defeat of federal structural reform, especially in the area of Medicaid.[31] A few of these state efforts are reviewed briefly below.

Hawaii

In 1974 Hawaii passed an employer-mandate health insurance law that covers half of the state's population. Virtual universal coverage is assured by Medicaid for the non-employed and by the State Health Insurance programme that covers persons not eligible for Medicaid who are not covered by employment-tied plans.[32] These programmes recently moved to a managed care model.[33]

Massachusetts

In 1988 Massachusetts enacted legislation that by 1992 was to assure affordable medical insurance for all state residents, either through workplace coverage or through a state plan, with the costs paid by those employers who did not provide workplace coverage.[34] Political change caused the programme to be repeatedly delayed and then rescinded before it went into effect.

Oregon

In 1989 Oregon enacted a reform of its Medicaid programme to expand eligibility to an additional 100,000 persons (over the 200,000 covered by Medicaid at that time), by reducing costs through prioritizing services. A number of publications have appeared on the details of the methods.[35] Briefly, the initial method was flawed and the list was revised to be more intuitive to the public. The list was used to price capitated contracts to managed care plans. The programme has been implemented, but the expansion of Medicaid to cover a higher proportion of the uninsured has been delayed.

Minnesota

In 1992 Minnesota enacted a reform to cover about one-half of the uninsured in the state through subsidized enrolment in integrated service networks – local networks of hospitals and physicians receiving payment from the state and members. Reforms on the rating and underwriting practices for small employers were also enacted.[36] Implementation was delayed until 1997.

Payer–provider initiatives

Both payers and providers are responding to the market-driven structural changes and state government Medicaid experiments. They can be grouped into three categories: managed care, corporate restructuring, and integrated systems.

Managed care is continuing to grow. In a few states 70 per cent of the insured under-65 population and 25 per cent of the over-65 population are in managed care plans. Managed care plans are merging across states, and more than a dozen multi-state plans have more than one million members. Managed care plans are branching out into Medicare and Medicaid contracts. Managed care plans are also moving into claims processing for self-insured employers and purchasing of traditional health insurance carriers to offer point-of-service choice and preferred provider options.[37] Point-of-service choice models are the fastest growing option with the employers' community.

A second element of 'reform without reform' is the corporate restructuring of the practice of medicine. One fear of the medical community was that the governmental reforms would reduce their autonomy. Now, physicians have to fear that for-profit corporations will reduce their autonomy. A number of organizations have emerged that are purchasing physician practices and operating multi-specialty groups. The physicians become salaried employees of these firms, who specialize in capitation contracts with managed care plans. The issues of productivity and compliance with appropriateness standards become paramount in such arrangements, leading to the deprofessionalization of medicine that was a feared outcome of reform.[38]

A third element is the development of closed integrated delivery systems. In some ways a return to the original prepaid group practices like Kaiser-Permanente, these systems combine the HMO concept with hospitals, home health care, primary care physician groups, and multi-specialty referral clinics either under unified ownership or through a long-term alliance among distinct organizsations.[39] Unlike Kaiser-Permanente, these integrated systems are not created to serve a defined membership, but rather consist of the hospitals, physicians and managed care plans in a community coalescing into long-term strategic alliances. In a number of cities such as Minneapolis-St. Paul (Minnesota), Albuquerque (New Mexico), Portland (Oregon), and Sacramento and San Diego (California) three integrated systems have emerged, with every hospital and managed care plan and most physicians aligned to one of the systems.[40] The long-term effect of oligopolistic health care markets will be interesting to observe. Market competition may require more government regulation, if three-firm oligopolies become the norm in most US urban markets.

CONCLUSIONS

Health care politics in America and the prospects for future reform appear to be very dim. What are the implications for other countries?

First, cherish your universal coverage and relatively lower costs. You may not realize how good your systems really are. Second, cherish your commitment to solidarity and equity. Your systems may lack efficiency from the perspective of health economists who are concerned with moral hazard and cross-subsidization from the young and healthy to the old and sick, but that is the price for a sense of community and social justice.

Third, be very careful about the creation of a large upper tier of persons who purchase all of their care privately, not simply supplementing their NHS or NHI services with non-essential care or queue-jumping insurance. A dangerous political dynamic can be created if a large segment of the population leaves a primary care gatekeeping structure for direct access to specialists. Support for the public system could decline, and with it funding for the public system.

Fourth, be even more careful about moving to a three tier system – that blurs the issues even more, and leads to greater fragmentation and loss of cost control. Fifth (this is for members of the European Union), do not even attempt to create a uniform system of health care financing and delivery within the EU. Accept that coverage and benefits will vary widely across Europe.

NOTES

1 P. Starr (1982) *The Social Transformation of American Medicine.* New York: Basic Books; E. Friedman (1986) Fifty years of US health care policy. *Hospitals,* 60 (9): 95–104; A.R. Somers (1986) The changing demand for health services: A historical perspective and some thoughts for the future. *Inquiry,* 23 (4): 395–402; B. B. Longest, Jr. (1988) American health policy in the year 2000. *Hospitals and Health Services Administration,* 33 (4): 419–34; R. Stevens (1989) *In Sickness and In Wealth: American Hospitals in the Twentieth Century.* New York: Basic Books; N. Goldfield (1994) The looming fight over health care reform: What we can learn from past debates. *Health Care Management Review,* 19 (3): 70–80; H. Helco (1995) The Clinton health plan: Historical perspective. *Health Affairs,* 14 (1): 86–98; T. Skocpol (1995) The rise and resounding demise of the Clinton plan. *Health Affairs,* 14 (1): 66–85.

2 D.J. Rothman (1993) A century of failure: Health care reform in America. *Journal of Health Politics, Policy and Law,* 18 (2): 271–86.
3 C. Tokarski (1990) 1980s prove uncertainty of instant cures. *Modern Healthcare,* 20 (1): 51–8.
4 R. Coile, Jr. (1990) No consensus, no vision for the nineties. *Healthcare Forum Journal,* 33 (6): 103–5.
5 J.D. Rockefeller, IV. (1990) The Pepper Commission report on comprehensive health care. *New England Journal of Medicine,* 323 (14): 1005–7; L. Wagner (1990) Pepper panel's healthcare blueprint omits funding, bipartisan support. *Modern Healthcare,* 20 (10): 20–4.
6 R.C. Coile, Jr. (1990) Technology and ethics: Three scenarios for the 1990s. *Quality Review Bulletin,* 16 (6): 202–8; R.B. Donker and J.A. Ogilvy (1993) The iron triangle and the chrome pentagon. *Health Forum Journal,* 36 (6): 72–7.
7 B. Starfield (1993) Primary care. *Journal of Ambulatory Care Management,* 16 (4): 27–37; B. Starfield (1993) Primary care as part of US health services reform. *Journal of the American Medical Association,* 269 (24): 3136–9.
8 U.E. Reinhardt (1995) Turning our gaze from bread and circus games. *Health Affairs,* 14 (1): 3–36.
9 M.V. Paul and J.C. Goodman (1995) Tax credits for health insurance and medical savings accounts. *Health Affairs,* 14(1): 126–39; S.M. Butler (1995) The conservative agenda for incremental reform. *Health Affairs,* 14 (1): 150–60.
10 M. Friedman (1991) Gammon's law points to health care solution. *Wall Street Journal,* B1+, November 21.
11 R.G. Davis (1985) Congress and the emergence of public health policy. *Health Care Management Review,* 10 (1): 61–73.
12 H.M. Culbertson and G.H. Stempel, III (1985) 'Media Malaise': Explaining personal optimism and societal pessimism about health care. *Journal of Communication,* 35 (2): 180–90; C. Jajich-Toth and B. W. Roper (1990) American views on health care: A study in contradictions. *Health Affairs,* 9 (4): 149–57.
13 M. Schlesinger and T-K. Lee (1993) Is health care different? Popular support of federal health and social policies. *Journal of Health Politics, Policy and Law,* 18 (3): 551–628.
14 G.D. Lundberg (1991) National health care reform: An aura of inevitability is upon us. *Journal of the American Medical Association,* 265 (19): 2566–7; G.D. Lundberg (1992) National health care reform: The aura of inevitability intensifies. *Journal of the American Medical Association,* 267 (18): 2521–4; H. Stout (1993) Most Americans pledge sacrifice to help fix the health system. *Wall Street Journal,* A1–A4, March 12.
15 B. Clinton (1992) The Clinton health care plan, *New England Journal of Medicine,* 327 (11): 804–6.
16 R. Resnick (1992) Health reform plans adapted from Jackson Hole vie for support. *Business and Health,* 10 (11): 41–4.

17 E. Weissenstein (1994) Last year's legacy for healthcare reform. *Modern Healthcare*, 24 (51): 42–4.

18 L. Wagner (1994) Reform resolution. *Modern Healthcare*, 24 (2): 34–40.

19 M. Podhorzer, L. Driscoll and E.S. Rothschild (1993) Unhealthy homey: The growth in health PAC's Congressional campaign contributions. *International Journal of Health Services*, 23 (1): 81–93.

20 V. Kemper and V. Novak (1993) What's blocking health care reform? *International Journal of Health Services*, 23 (1): 69–79.

21 J.M. Sharfstein and S.S. Sharfstein (1994) Campaign contributions from the American medical political action committee to members of Congress. *New England Journal of Medicine*, 330 (1): 32–7.

22 L. Wagner and E. Weissenstein (1992) As healthcare groups help fill campaign coffers, the question is: What is the money buying? *Modern Healthcare*, 22 (44): 38–40.

23 J. Frieden (1992) Lobbyists want to limit federal intervention in health care. *Business and Health*, 10 (10): 46–9.

24 M. Weir (1995) Institutional and political obstacles to reform. *Health Affairs*, 14 (1): 102–4.

25 U.E. Reinhardt (1992) Politics and the health care system. *New England Journal of Medicine*, 327 (11): 809–11; D. Yankelovich (1995) The debate that wasn't: The public and the Clinton plan. *Health Affairs*, 14 (1): 7–23.

26 S.J. Wesbury, Jr. (1990) Why Other Nations' RX Won't Work. *Healthcare Executive*, 5 (4): 17–19.

27 E. Ginsberg (1988) US health policy – Expectation and realities. *Journal of American Medical Association*, 260 (24): 3647–50; R.D. Lamm (1988) An eight-count indictment against America. *Medical Group Management Journal*, 35 (4): 21–4; V.R. Fuchs (1992) The best health care system in the world. *Journal of American Medical Association*, 268 (7): 916–17.

28 L.C. Thurow (1985) Medicine versus economics. *New England Journal of Medicine*, 313 (10): 611–14.

29 O.W. Anderson (1990) Letter to the Editor. *Hospitals and Health Services Administration*, 35 (3): 305–7; D. Blumentahl (1991) The timing and course of health care reform. *New England Journal of Medicine*, 325 (3): 198–200; E. Ginzberg (1995) The restructuring of the US health care system. *Inquiry*, 22 (3): 272–81; J.J. Mongan (1995) Anatomy and physiology of health reforms' failure. *Health Affairs*, 14 (1): 99–101.

30 M.S. Dukakis and S. Michael (1992) The states and health care reform. *New England Journal of Medicine*, 327 (15): 1090–2; M. Moon and J. Holahan (1992) Can the states take the lead in health care reform? *Journal of the American Medical Association*, 268 (12): 1588–94; J. Johnsson (1992) State health reform. *Hospitals*, 66 (19): 26–38.

31 Sany Lutz (1995) For real reform watch the states. *Modern Healthcare*, 25 (3): 35–6.

32 General Accounting Office (1994) *Health Care in Hawaii*. Washington, DC: US General Accounting Office (GAO/HEHS-94-68).

33 L. Kertesz (1995) New Hawaiian program suffers growing pains. *Modern Healthcare*, 25 (3): 35–6.
34 S.A. Goldberger (1990) The politics of universal access: The Massachusetts Health Security Act of 1988. *Journal of Health Politics, Policy and Law*, 15 (4): 857–85; R. Kronick (1990) The slippery slope of health care finance: Business interests and hospital reimbursement in Massachusetts. *Journal of Health Politics, Policy and Law*, 15 (4): 887–913.
35 D.M. Eddy (1991) Oregon's methods. *Journal of the American Medical Association*, 266 (15): 2135–41; D.C. Hadorn (1991) Setting health care priorities in Oregon. *Journal of the American Medical Association*, 265 (17): 2218–25; R.M. Kaplan (1993) *The Hippocratic Predicament*. San Diego, CA: Academic Press.
36 S. H. Miles, N. Lurie, L. Quam and A. Caplan (1992) Health care reform in Minnesota. *New England Journal of Medicine*, 327 (15): 1092–5; T. Hudson (1994) Tailgating the market. *Hospitals and Health Networks*, 68 (11): 34–40.
37 P.J. Kenkel (1993) Managed-care firms star in third-party roles. *Modern Healthcare*, 23 (1): 31–41.
38 S.A. Freedman (1985) Megacorporate health care. *New England Journal of Medicine*, 312 (9): 579–82; R.R. Reed and D. Evans (1987) The deprofessionalization of Medicine. *Journal of the American Medical Association*, 258 (22): 3279–82.
39 D.E.L. Johnson (1993) Integrated systems face major hurdles, regulations. *Health Care Strategic Management*, 11 (10): 2–3.
40 R.C. Coile, Jr. (1993) Three-system towns. *Healthcare Forum Journal*, 36 (1): 87.

3

THE UNITED KINGDOM
Chris Ham

INTRODUCTION

In a number of developed countries, policy makers are introducing reforms to the financing and delivery of health service.[1] Among these countries, change has progressed furthest and fastest in the United Kingdom. The reforms to the NHS stem from a review initiated by Prime Minister Margaret Thatcher in 1988. The proximate cause of the review was a perceived crisis in the funding of public hospitals. During the autumn of 1987, a number of hospitals had to make reductions in staffing and beds in order to keep expenditure within budget. This led to a series of well publicized cases of children being denied heart operations because of the shortages of resources and specialist facilities. The leaders of the medical profession issued a statement calling for an analysis of how additional and alternative funds for health care might be raised and as a short-term measure extra public money was allocated to deal with the problem. In parallel, Margaret Thatcher announced that she was establishing a fundamental review of the NHS and its future and that the results would be published within a year.

Beyond the immediate funding problems of hospitals lay a series of more fundamental pressures which contributed to the setting up of the Thatcher review. These included the existence of long waiting times for non-urgent hospital treatment, the uneven quality of care for elderly people and people with mental illness and learning disabilities, and evidence of wide variations in performance within the NHS. The last of these points was highlighted in a speech by the Secretary of State for Health at the time the Thatcher review was launched:

Some districts treat only 25 patients per year in each surgical bed while others manage 53. Even when adjusted to take into account differences between the patients treated, some districts are still treating 14 per cent fewer patients than would be expected, while others are treating 27 per cent more.

Similarly, there are districts with an average length of stay 13 per cent longer than expected while others manage a length of stay almost 22 per cent less than expected.

And if we turn to costs we again find large variations. Costs within any one group of similar districts can vary by as much as 50 per cent...

So despite the Health Service's unquestionable achievements in boosting efficiency, I am convinced there is room for yet more improvements in performance.[2]

While these variations had been known about for some time, evidence of this kind was invoked to justify a wide ranging analysis of how the NHS could be improved.

THE THATCHER REVIEW

In the event, the Thatcher review came down against major changes to the financing of the NHS. In the white paper setting out the results of the review, *Working for Patients*, the government reaffirmed its commitment to a health service funded out of taxation and delivering comprehensive health care to the entire population.[3] This followed from an assessment of alternative models of funding in other countries which led senior ministers to conclude that there would be no inherent advantage in moving away from a single payer system.[4] Having decided not to change the financing system, the Thatcher review focused on how the delivery of health services could be strengthened. It was this that led to proposals to create a so called 'internal market' in health care. These proposals can be traced back to an analysis undertaken by Alain Enthoven in the mid-1980s, but they were also consistent with changes introduced into other parts of the public sector by the Thatcher government.[5]

The debate surrounding *Working for Patients* was intense. The government's proposals were strongly opposed by the medical and nursing professions as well as opposition parties who argued that they would undermine the principles on which the NHS was established. Criticism focused particularly on plans to introduce competition between health care providers. It was argued that this would threaten the achievement of equity and access in the NHS and result in the commercialization of health care. Unfavourable parallels were drawn with the United States, critics arguing that the achievement of the NHS in delivering comprehensive health services to the whole population at low cost was being put at risk, and that the UK was moving inexorably towards a mixed economy of health care in which costs would rise and patients would suffer as the role of the private health care sector increased.

In fact, the Thatcher government's proposals affected the private health care sector only indirectly. As far as health care financing was concerned, tax relief on private health insurance was made available to people aged over 60, at the Prime Minister's insistence and in the face of opposition of senior cabinet colleagues, but the effect of this was marginal. Much more significant, at least potentially, was the opportunity available to private hospitals to compete for contracts to deliver services to NHS patients. Although the NHS reforms are often described as involving an internal market, in reality it is open to private providers as well as public providers to bid for business from those purchasing care on behalf of patients. It was this, more than the incentives offered to older people to take out private insurance, that lay behind many of the claims that the NHS was on the road to privatization. Competition between public and private providers for NHS resources is however closely regulated and it would be more accurate to describe the reforms as leading to a managed market in health care rather than an internal market.

Notwithstanding the strength of opposition to *Working for Patients*, the Thatcher government was able to use its large parliamentary majority to pass its proposals into law in 1990 and implementation of the reforms started in 1991. In the five years that have elapsed since then, the organization and management of the NHS have been transformed.[6] Of particular significance has been the move away from the integration of responsibility for financing and managing services in health authorities to a separation of purchaser and provider roles. This has created the conditions for providers to compete with each other for resources from purchasers and has challenged the traditional power of providers to direct the development of publicly financed health care systems. Put another way, policy makers are seeking to tackle the problems of provider capture (even though they would not use this language) by establishing a countervailing force in the shape of purchasing organizations able to hold providers accountable for their performance.

This reflects belated recognition in political circles of what has long been recognized in academic research, namely that even in systems of socialized medicine it is health care professionals and providers who have traditionally exerted most influence.[7]

In the reformed NHS, the integration of functions in district health authorities has been replaced gradually with a separation of purchaser and provider roles. This has been achieved by the creation of new institutions, NHS trusts, to take responsibility for the management of hospital and community health services. By 1996, almost all NHS services in England were run as trusts. The establishment of trusts has enabled health authorities to concentrate on purchasing services for the populations they serve. These changes have gone hand in hand with a new way of allocating resources within the NHS. Instead of being funded to provide services in their hospitals, health authorities are now allocated resources to buy services for the people who live in their area. This means that health authority budgets are no longer adjusted for cross-boundary patient flows but are based solely on the size of the population served weighted for age, sex and other relevant factors. The cost of treating patients outside the district of residence is met by the health authority where patients live.

Alongside the population based approach to purchasing of health authorities, the NHS reforms have introduced a patient based model in the form of general practitioner fundholding. This involves groups of GPs holding a budget with which they purchase a limited range of services for their patients. Initially, the rules specified that only practices with 11,000 patients or more would be eligible to apply to become fundholders in England. This limit was subsequently reduced to 7000 patients and then to 3000 patients. At the same time encouragement was given to smaller practices to become fundholders by linking up with larger practices and by collaborating in networks that have become known as multifunds. Fundholding is a voluntary scheme and by April 1996 it covered over 50 per cent of the population in England.

The scope of fundholding has been extended progressively. To begin with, it covered a defined range of hospital services, the cost of drugs, and an allowance for practice staff. Taken together, these services comprised around 20 per cent of the hospital and community health services used by patients. In 1993 a number of community services were added, and in 1994, GPs in a few areas took responsibility for the total budget for their patients on an experimental basis. The existence of GP fundholding alongside health

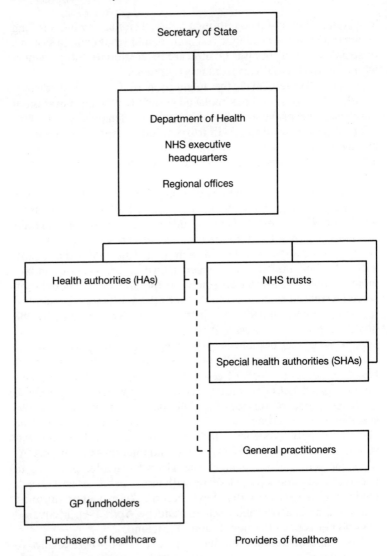

Figure 3.1 New structure of the NHS

authorities has had the effect of introducing a degree of competition among purchasers as each kind of purchaser seeks to demonstrate its ability to negotiate improvements in services for patients.
This has been reinforced by a funding arrangement in which the

budgets of fundholders are deducted from resources controlled by health authorities.

The move away from an integrated system has led to the introduction of contracts or service agreements to provide the link between purchasers and providers. The purpose of contracts is to specify the cost, quality and quantity of care that should be provided. NHS contracts are not legal documents but are management devices for codifying the agreements made by purchasers and providers. The architects of the reforms hoped that through contracts money would follow the patient. This was intended to create an incentive for providers to respond to the demands of patients and those purchasing care on their behalf.

These then are the basic building blocks in the reformed NHS. In seeking to assess the impact of the reforms, independent analysts are hampered by the absence of evaluative research. The Thatcher government steadfastly refused to commission studies into the effects of the reforms and it has therefore been left to independent foundations and other funding agencies to fill the gap. Of particular note in this context is the research sponsored by the King's Fund which has resulted in a series of reports on particular aspects of the reforms.[8] This research, together with work carried out by other analysts and the author's own involvement in studying the evolution of the reforms, enables a preliminary assessment of their impact to be made.[9] Nevertheless, it must be recognized that interpretation of the available evidence continues to be contested and the policy of implementing the reforms in stages means that data drawn from the early phases of implementation may not reflect accurately the way in which the changes develop in the longer term. With this warning in mind, we now consider the development of competition in the UK health service and the effect on patients and providers.

THE REFORMS IN ACTION: 1991–96

In the first year of the reforms, the government sought to ensure that change was introduced in a planned fashion. In the code language favoured by politicians and civil servants, the emphasis was placed on a 'steady state' and a 'smooth take off' for the reforms. This meant that competition was slow to develop except in London where the existence of many acute hospitals in close proximity to each other created the circumstances in which purchasers had significant opportunities to switch contracts between providers. This was reinforced by the introduction of a formula for funding purchasers based on the population served rather than the services managed (see above). Health authorities in inner London where the population was declining lost resources to health authorities in the Home Counties where the population was growing. Given the historical concentration of hospital and specialist services in inner London, this had an immediate and dramatic impact. Resources and contracts flowed away from the relatively expensive teaching hospitals in the inner cities to acute hospitals in surrounding areas with lower costs and greater accessibility.

The funding problems this created led the government to set up an independent inquiry in 1991 chaired by Professor Sir Bernard Tomlinson to review the future of health services in London and make recommendations. The problems of London were reflected in other conurbations, albeit to a lesser extent and at a slower pace. It became clear from these developments that one of the most significant effects of the NHS reforms would be to force a rationalization of acute hospitals in the major cities. This went alongside a policy of giving greater priority to primary care and community health services in order to compensate for the reduction of hospital services and to enable more health problems to be dealt with in the community.

The example of London is instructive. It illustrates that the signals thrown up by the market were joined with an independent overview in an attempt to ensure an orderly process of change. Additional resources were made available to hospitals in the London area to enable them to balance their budgets while the direction of change was debated and agreed. Following publication of the Tomlinson report in 1992, the government published its own proposals for change and commissioned further reviews into the provision of specialist services and research.[10] In addition, the London Implementation Group was set up to oversee the closure of hospitals and the rationalization of services. Taken together, these measures represented an attempt to manage the market and to ensure that the interests of patients did not suffer during a programme of substantial change.

As in the original debate on the NHS reforms, the review of health services in London provoked strong opposition among those most affected and led to concerted campaigns to protect famous institutions under threat, such as St Bartholomew's Hospital. Equally important, the analysis on which the planned reductions in hospital services was based was criticized for failing to take into account factors such as the availability of nursing home and residential care provision.[11] In the event, although health ministers made some concessions to their critics and did not implement the recommendations of the Tomlinson report in full, the broad thrust of the report was accepted and led to a major programme of change in London. This included a reduction in the number of hospitals and beds, the merger of medical schools, a concentration of specialist expertise and research capacity, and a programme of investment in primary care amounting to £140 million.

Across the NHS as a whole, the most important impact of the reforms was to change the balance of power between different interests. In organizational terms, the old hierarchical integrated structures have been replaced by a more diverse set of contractual arrangements. Within these arrangements, the traditional power of providers, especially those based in acute hospitals, has been challenged. This was driven by the transformation of health authorities from provider oriented organizations to become purchasers of services for local people. In their new purchasing role, health authorities work closely with GPs to decide what services to buy and where to place contracts. This reflects the key position of GPs as gatekeepers to hospital services. The position of GPs in relation to their hospital colleagues was considerably enhanced by these developments and a capacity was created for examining the population's need for health care independently of the management of health care institutions.

Public health directors employed by health authorities were important figures in this process. The annual reports produced by public health directors painted a picture of health in each district and identified the major causes of premature mortality and morbidity. The importance of the public health perspective was reinforced by publication by the Major government of a health strategy for England.[12] This set out national targets for improving health and identified health authorities as the agencies at a local level with lead responsibility for ensuring that these targets were achieved. Over a period of time, these developments had the effect of changing the emphasis within health authorities from the management of providers to the health needs of populations.

This change did not happen quickly and in many districts there was still a perception that health authorities remained wedded to their former responsibilities as providers. But the separation of purchaser and provider roles coupled with the development of the national health strategy and the importance attached to the health needs assessment responsibility of health authorities provided the basis for a progressive re-examination of health care priorities and established patterns of resource distribution. Not least, it challenged the priority that had traditionally been given to acute hospital services and led to a renewed interest in health promotion, primary care and community services. On an annual basis, decision making in district health authorities continued to be characterized by incrementalism but over a period of time it became clear that there was an opportunity to think afresh about priorities and to question the traditional power of the acute sector.[13]

Nowhere was this shift in the balance of power better illustrated than in relation to GP fundholding. With the budgets to back their decisions, fundholders were well placed to negotiate service improvements for their patients.[14] The evidence indicates that they did this in a number of ways, including offering extra services in their practices, reducing waiting times for outpatient appointments and elective surgery, and improving communication with hospital doctors and managers. As experience showed, the importance of fundholding was twofold: first, it promoted changes to the delivery of acute services; and second, it prompted a review of what could be done in primary care. The latter included examination of policies on the prescribing of drugs, referrals to hospitals by GPs, and the scope for increasing the range of services delivered in a primary care setting. In many cases, this resulted in fundholders employing additional staff such as physiotherapists, dieticians and counsellors, arranging for hospital specialists to see patients in their own clinics rather than in hospital, and working more closely with colleagues involved in the provision of community care.

Despite these changes, opinions on fundholding in the medical profession were strongly divided. Also there were concerns that in the long term the expansion of fundholding would undermine the ability of health authorities to plan and purchase services from a population perspective. The emergence of hybrid models of purchasing in which health authorities worked closely with GPs in carrying out their responsibilities added a further layer of complexity, suggesting that it might be possible to combine the sensitivity to patients of GPs with the public health focus of health authorities in a way which distilled the most positive features of each model.[15] An alternative school of thought was that the purchasing function was becoming increasingly fragmented and that this would make it more difficult to challenge the power of providers and introduce planned change.

One of the immediate effects of the growing power of purchasers and GPs was to stimulate a reorientation on the part of providers. NHS trusts, particularly those operating in competitive environments, were not slow to perceive the risks they faced if they failed to respond to the demands of purchasers. To this extent, the shift away from a funding system based on prospective global budgets to one in which the income of providers accrued from contracts negotiated with purchasers had a significant impact on the behaviour of those involved in acute hospitals. Among other changes, it led hospital managers and clinicians to market their services actively to purchasers and GPs and to assess their strengths and weaknesses in relation to competitors. Put another way, providers became more outward looking, less preoccupied with internal problems and focused increasingly on the demands of their customers and those purchasing care for them. These developments were accelerated by the increasing interest shown by private providers in winning contracts from NHS purchasers. While private providers achieved some success in this respect, overall the vast majority of contracts remained within the NHS. Indeed, NHS trusts began competing more aggressively for private income, leading to complaints that private providers were at a disadvantage in the managed market.[16]

As implementation of the reforms progressed, it became apparent that a system based on contracts was more expensive to administer than one based on integration. The scale of increase in management costs was difficult to quantify with precision but there was little doubt that more managers had to be employed to negotiate and monitor contracts and to supply the information needed by both purchasers and providers. Fundholding accentuated this problem by establishing a large number of small purchasers alongside health authorities whose numbers were steadily reduced by a process of mergers and amalgamations. The workload for NHS trusts in negotiating contracts with a range of purchasers each with different cost and quality requirements was considerable and at times threatened to drown those involved in a sea of paper. In view of these developments, it came as no surprise that in 1993 the government initiated a review of the organization of the NHS and its management costs with a view to streamlining the structure of the NHS and cutting back on unnecessary bureaucracy.[17]

The impact of the reforms on patients is more difficult to assess.

One of the distinctive contributions made to the reforms by Prime Minister John Major was publication of the *Patient's Charter*.[18] This was one of a series of charters published by the Major government in an effort to make more explicit the rights of public service users. In the case of the NHS, the *Patient's Charter* established standards for the reduction of waiting times for hospital treatment and it set out a range of rights including the right to be registered with a GP and to be referred to a hospital specialist when a GP considered this to be necessary. This policy had some success in that the longest waiting times for treatment were reduced but to some degree this was at the expense of an increase in the number of patients waiting for relatively short periods of time. It should also be noted that a significant cause of the waiting time reductions that did occur was the strong pressure applied by health ministers. Managers and chairpersons of health authorities were told that their jobs were at risk if waiting times were not brought into line with the *Patient's Charter* and it was this, more than the introduction of competition between providers, that was mainly responsible for the improvements that occurred.

A claim often made by health ministers was that the reforms had led to an increase in productivity with more patients being treated than ever before. On the face of it, this claim had some validity, with official figures showing an increase in the number of patients treated of 21 per cent between 1991 and 1994.[19] However, behind these figures lay improvements in recording arrangements as NHS trusts modernized their information systems in the process of implementing the reforms. The increase in productivity also coincided with a period in which the NHS was more generously funded than in the past and this probably contributed to the extra activity that occurred.[20] A further factor to bear in mind is that there was a change in the way in which patient activity in hospitals was classified and this led some analysts to argue that the productivity gains cited by government spokespersons were artificially inflated.[21]

One of the original objectives of *Working for Patients* was to increase patient choice and to make services more responsive to patients. It was for this reason that the architects of the reforms hoped to develop a system in which money would follow the patient. In practice, health authorities used mainly block contracts with their providers and these were insensitive to increases in productivity or quality. As a consequence, patients tended to follow the money rather than vice versa and this served to restrict choice. GP fundholders were an exception to this and for the range of services they purchased were able to decide with patients on the provider to be used. But with fundholding covering a minority of the population and only a defined list of services, its impact was limited. Patient choice of GP was not affected by the reforms and indeed may even have been enhanced by the requirement that GPs should publish more information about the services they offered. On balance, independent assessments concluded that the reforms had had a marginal effect on patient choice and certainly did not result in the kinds of changes envisaged by those involved in the Thatcher review.[22]

Responsiveness to patients is a more elusive concept. The waiting time for hospital treatment is one aspect of responsiveness and trends in this area have already been reviewed. Beyond this, there is little systematic evidence on which to judge. A report by the Health Services Commissioner or Ombudsman published in 1994 was critical of the record of the NHS in responding to patient complaints and argued that the more fragmented structure introduced as a consequence of the reforms had made it difficult to coordinate the provision of care.[23] Against this, there was evidence in some areas that certain services were being provided more accessibly, for example through hospital specialists seeing patients in GPs' clinics, and that levels of dissatisfaction with the NHS on the part of the public were declining.[24] In truth, raising the standards of health care was an issue high on the health policy agenda right through the 1980s and it was difficult to sustain the argument that the reforms *per se* were responsible for any improvements in this area.[25]

ANALYSIS

In view of the relatively short period that has elapsed since the reforms were introduced, it would be premature to draw firm conclusions on their impact. Nevertheless, it is possible to identify some tentative lessons and to indicate the strengths and weaknesses of the arrangements that have been put in place.

To begin with, it is apparent that the changes to the NHS have unlocked established relationships. The providers of acute hospital services who have traditionally exerted a great deal of influence over the development of health care have found their own position under challenge by an alliance of purchasers and GPs. This is resulting in a major rationalization of acute service provision in cities such as London. Outside these cities, purchasers and GPs, including fundholders, are using their leverage to hold providers more accountable for their performance. At the same time, they are examining the scope for strengthening services in primary care, community health services and prevention. Acute sector providers have responded to these developments by seeking to market their services more aggressively. The unlocking of established relationships has also opened up new opportunities for services to be developed in different ways and for the traditional division between primary care and secondary care to be bridged. This is illustrated by the provision of specialist clinics in GPs' premises, the development of shared care protocols for the joint management of patients with chronic conditions such as asthma and diabetes by GPs and specialists, and an extension of the role of GPs into hospitals in some areas, particularly in relation to accident and emergency services (in inner cities), minor surgery and long-term and convalescent care. None of these developments is entirely new but all have been accelerated by recent changes.

The key element in the reforms that has stimulated these developments is the separation of purchaser and provider roles. The new mindset introduced by purchasers has brought into question the long-term dominance of acute hospital providers and has offered a fresh way of thinking about the population's health needs. As time has gone on, it has become clear that the role of a purchaser is quite different from that of a conventional health insurer. Purchasers do not simply reimburse providers for delivering care to patients but are actively involved in determining needs and the most appropriate way of responding to those needs. This involves questioning the cost effectiveness of services and targeting scarce resources where they will achieve the most health gain for the population served. It also means focusing on health as well as health services and working in alliance with other agencies to tackle the conditions outside the health sector which have such an important influence on health status.

This combination of responsibilities means that purchasers are much more than simply payers. They are organizations which, at their best, bring together expertise in public health, general management, planning, finance, and community participation and achieve strategic change through the use of their financial and other resources. The full potential of population based purchasing has yet to be realized, and it has taken time to shift away from a provider dominated culture. But the establishment of purchasing organizations whose responsibilities cover both the hospital and community health services and family health services in 1996 holds out the prospect of a further shift away from acute based care, and the opportunity to strengthen primary and community services.

If there is a question mark over these developments, it arises because of the unanticipated obstacles that may have been created through the institutional separation of purchaser and provider roles. The establishment of NHS trusts to take responsibility for service provision has had the positive effect of liberating health authorities to concentrate on the population's health needs but at the same time it has put an organizational boundary around the existing pattern of service provision. Paradoxically, this may make it harder to achieve some of the service changes which are required in future – just as the need to make these changes has become more urgent. The very act of creating organizations who will judge their own success by their ability to survive (at a minimum) and expand may run counter to the objectives of purchasers, whether health authorities or fundholders.

Although the NHS reforms have already resulted in a number of mergers between trusts, these usually occur only when no other alternative is available. It follows that purchasers may have difficulty in stimulating the development of innovations in service delivery unless they can carry providers with them. Given a long tradition of provider dominance, it would be unrealistic to expect a fundamental change of approach even though purchasers are rapidly learning how to use the new levers they have available. Add to this the increase in transaction costs involved in shifting from an integrated approach to a contract based system, and the long-term benefits of separating purchaser and provider roles become questionable.

What then of GP fundholding? In some respects, this is the most innovative aspect of all the changes taking place and the one that has attracted the greatest attention. Variously described as the wild card or winning hand,[26] fundholding forces even the most dispassionate observer off the fence. By giving primary care providers responsibility for running a budget, fundholding contaminates the purity of the separation of purchaser and provider roles. It also gives GPs a strong incentive to undertake more work themselves, thereby reducing the use of and expenditure on other services. This strength is at the same time a potential weakness in creating a risk that patients will be undertreated because of the financial imperatives built into fundholding. In recognition of this, the rules surrounding the scheme seek to prohibit GPs from benefiting personally from any savings made, and the research carried out so far has uncovered no systematic evidence either of risk selection or cream skimming. Despite this, and notwithstanding the benefits that fundholders have brought about on behalf of their patients, doubts persist about the viability and indeed desirability of fundholding in the longer term.

In so far as generalizations are possible, it can be argued that a combination of the patient perspective of GPs and the population focus of health authorities may be more effective as an agent of change than either model operating independently. This might be achieved through health authorities holding the entire budget and seeking the advice of GPs on how this budget should be used, or by GPs taking responsibility for purchasing all services for their patients but under the umbrella of a health authority charged with a strategic planning role. At present, neither of these approaches seems likely to emerge in pure form and it is probable that in the foreseeable future a variety of models will exist in different parts of the UK.[27] Unless steps are taken to achieve synchronized purchasing by health authorities and fundholders, there is a real risk of fragmentation and harmful instability.

Not least, one of the great strengths of the NHS, the availability of a district general hospital providing a full range of services in each locality, will be under threat if fundholders resort to shopping around for the best deals for their patients regardless of where these deals are obtained. Again, the indications on this point are contradictory, with fundholders in some areas remaining loyal to their local providers and working with them to improve performance, while fundholders in other areas prefer to engage in 'spot purchasing' from a range of providers in the public and private sectors. The risk of fragmentation is of course the other side of the coin of the loosening of sclerotic relationships. This suggests the need to strike a balance between the two in a managed market which combines the incentives for improved performance of a competitive approach and the stability associated with planning and regulation.

In recognition of this, a framework for market management was published at the end of 1994.[28] This acknowledged the requirement that competition should be regulated and set out a series of rules for handling purchaser mergers, provider mergers, situations in which providers experience financial difficulty, and collusion and anti-competitive behaviour. At around the same time, the government's plans for the future of purchasing were announced.[29] These involve an extension of GP fundholding and a new role for health authorities as the strategic commissioners of health services. It is envisaged that health authorities will continue to be involved in purchasing themselves but this responsibility will diminish in importance as the number of fundholders increases and as they purchase a wider range of care for patients. In order to avoid fragmentation of the purchasing function, the government's plans include an accountability framework intended to ensure that the activities of fundholders are coordinated with those of health authorities.

What impact these developments will have remains uncertain. During the course of 1994, the Secretary of State for Health, Virginia Bottomley, drew attention to the influence of developments in health care technology on hospital provision. In so doing, she raised the possibility of a 40 per cent reduction in acute hospital beds by the early part of the twenty-first century.[30] In practice, of course, the nature of hospital services that eventually emerges will be the outcome of the interplay of two sets of factors: the changes in health care technology referred to by the Secretary of State, and the financial and organizational arrangements put in place by policy makers. The unanswered question is whether the separation of purchaser and provider roles, the development of managed markets, and the establishment of population based and patient focused models of purchasing will facilitate or hinder the service changes made possible by developments in technology. The evidence presented in this chapter does not offer a simple answer to this question. While it is clear that the scope for introducing planned changes in service provision has been reduced, it is much less certain whether the creation of pluralistic, contract based arrangements will be a more powerful force for change than the hierarchical integrated structures they have replaced. On this fundamental question, the jury is still out.

NOTES

1 C.J. Ham, R. Robinson and M. Benzeval (1990) *Health Check*. London: King's Fund Institute; OECD (1992) *The Reform of Health Care: A Comparative Analysis of Seven OECD Countries*. Paris: OECD; C.J. Ham, and M. Brommels (1994) Health care reform in the Netherlands, Sweden and United Kingdom. *Health Affairs*, Winter: 106–19.

2 J. Moore (1988) *Protecting the Nation's Health*, Press Release 88/97. London: Department of Health and Social Security.

3 Secretary of State for Health and others (1989) *Working for Patients*. London: Her Majesty's Stationery Office.
4 N. Lawson (1992) *The View from No.11*. London: Bantam Press.
5 A. C. Enthoven (1985) *Reflections on the Management of the NHS*. London: Nuffield Provincial Hospitals Trust; P. Day and R. Klein (1991) Britain's Health Care Experiment. *Health Affairs*, Autumn: 39–59.
6 J. James (1994) *Transforming the NHS: The View from Inside*. Bath Centre for the Analysis of Social Policy, University of Bath.
7 R. Klein (1983) *The Politics of the National Health Service*. Longman: London.
8 R. Robinson and J. Le Grand (eds) (1994) *Evaluating the NHS Reforms*. London: King's Fund Institute.
9 J. Butler (1992) *Patients, Policies and Politics*. Buckingham: Open University Press; C.J. Ham (1994a) *Management and Competition in the New NHS*. Oxford: Radcliffe Medical Press.
10 B. Tomlinson (1992) *Report of the Inquiry into London's Health Services, Medical Education and Research*. London: Her Majesty's Stationery Office.
11 B. Jarman (1994) *The Crisis in London Medicine: How Many Hospital Beds Does the Capital Need?* London: University of London.
12 Secretary of State for Health (1992) *The Health of the Nation*. London: Her Majesty's Stationery Office.
13 R. Klein and S. Redmayne (1992) *Patterns of Priorities*. Birmingham: National Association of Health Authorities and Trusts.
14 H. Glennerster, M. Matsaganis and P. Owens with S. Hancock (1994) *Implementing GP Fundholding*. Buckingham: Open University Press.
15 J. Shapiro (1994) *Shared Purchasing and Collaborative Commissioning within the NHS*. Birmingham: National Association of Health Authorities and Trusts.
16 P. Jacobs (1994) Competition and co-operation in healthcare provision, in E. Butler (ed.). *Unhealthy Competition*. London: Adam Smith.
17 Department of Health (1993) *Managing the New NHS*. London: Department of Health.
18 Department of Health (1991) *The Patient's Charter*. London: Department of Health.
19 V. Bottomley (1994) Teamwork for health: Involving the public in the team, text of speech given at conference of the National Association of Health Authorities and Trusts, Bournemouth, June.
20 K. Bloor and A. Maynard (1993) *Expenditure on the NHS during and after the Thatcher Years*. York: Centre for Health Economics, University of York.
21 Radical Statistics Health Group (1992) NHS Reforms: The first six months – Proof of progress or a statistical smokescreen? *British Medical Journal*, 304: 705–9; Radical Statistics Health Group (1995) NHS 'indicators of success': What do they tell us? *British Medical Journal*, 310: 1045–50.

22 A. Mahon, D. Wilkin and C. Whitehouse (1994) Choice of hospital for elective surgery referrals: GPs' and patients' views, in R. Robinson and J. Le Grand (eds) *Evaluating the NHS Reforms*. London: King's Fund Institute.

23 Health Service Commissioner (1994) *Annual Report for 1993–94*. London: Her Majesty's Stationery Office.

24 R. Jowell, L. Brook and L. Dowd (eds) (1994) *British Social Attitudes*, 11th BSA Report. Aldershot: Dartmouth Publishing.

25 D. Jones, C. Lester and R. West (1994) Monitoring changes in health services for older people, in R. Robinson and J. Le Grand (eds) *Evaluating the NHS Reforms*. London: King's Fund Institute.

26 H. Glennerster, M. Matsaganis and P. Owens with S. Hancock (1994) *Implementing GP Fundholding*. Buckingham: Open University Press.

27 C. J. Ham (1994) 'The future of purchasing'. *British Medical Journal*, 309: 1032–3.

28 NHS Executive (1994) *The Operation of the Internal Market: Local Freedoms, National Responsibilities*. London: NHS Executive.

29 NHS Executive (1994) *Developing NHS Purchasing and GP Fundholding*. London: NHS Executive.

30 V. Bottomley (1994) Teamwork for health: Involving the public in the team, text of speech given at conference of the National Association of Health Authorities and Trusts, Bournemouth, June.

4

SWEDEN
Clas Rehnberg

INTRODUCTION

The health care system in Sweden has historically relied on planning and administrative coordination rather than market mechanisms. A fundamental principle is that all citizens should have the right to good health and equal access to health care regardless of where they live or their ability to pay for health services. The structure of the system can to a large extent be explained by its historical background. The county councils, which are part of local government, were established in the 1860s, mainly to operate hospitals for somatic illnesses. For out-patient care the structure was a combination of a state system of district physicians and private practitioners. Mental hospitals were managed and financed by central government. Over the last 25 years, several of the areas of responsibility of the central government have been transferred to the county councils which vary in size from 60,000 to 1.6 million inhabitants.

The main part of health care provision today is located in hospitals, primary health care centres and other facilities operated by the county councils. Most resources are used for in-house production. Contracted services with external (private) providers has been very limited. Private providers account for less than 10 per cent of total health care delivery, mainly in out-patient care. The system has had a somewhat monolithic structure with a similar way of delivering care in all county councils. The county councils are also empowered to impose a proportional income tax on their residents. Moreover, health care is essentially the county councils' only responsibility, accounting for 85–90 per cent of their operating costs.

The general health of the population is high. Life expectancy,

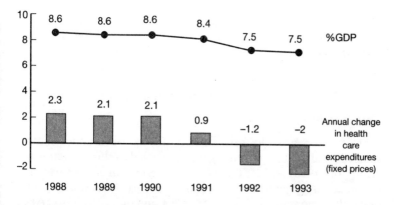

Figure 4.1 The development of health care expenditures as a share of GDP and annual changes of health care expenditures in fixed prices. *Source*: The Federation of the County Councils (1995)

infant and perinatal mortality statistics place Sweden among the healthiest countries in the world. However, it should be noted that these positive vital statistics cannot be attributed solely to the health care system. Regarding subtler measures, such as the quality of health care process and outcomes, and the attention paid to consumer preferences, the picture is less clear, although public opinion polls usually show that Swedish citizens rate their health care system highly.

During the past three decades health care has been one of the most rapidly expanding sectors in Sweden. From 1960 to 1982 health care expenditures rose continuously from 4.7 to 9.1 per cent of the gross domestic product (GDP). Health employment increased during the same period from 4.0 to 9.9 per cent of total employment. The major part of the expansion of health care took place in the public sector represented by the county councils. Central government had difficulties in controlling total health care costs, due to the decentralized structure of the system. Since 1985 health care expenditures as a percentage of GDP have been stable, with some reductions (Figure 4.1).[1]

Figure 4.1 shows the share of health care expenditures as a percentage of GDP and annual changes of health care expenditures in fixed prices. The larger part of this reduction is explained by the transfer of the responsibility for nursing homes from the county councils to the municipalities. However, the implementation of different reforms has taken place during a period with no real growth in the health care sector. In fact, efforts to cope with this constraint on real resources have led to a review of the efficiency, financing and organization of the system.

THE SITUATION BEFORE THE REFORMS

Cost containment

As stated above, health care expenditure has been under control since the mid-1980s. In the budget system used to allocate resources during the 1960s and 1970s, overspending by clinical departments was generally accepted by the county councils. After the introduction of frame or global budgets, a cap was put on expenditure. Also, central government controlled total expenditures by placing taxation limits on the county councils. Hence, it is important to note that cost containment was not a reason for reforming the system. Compared to other OECD countries, Sweden has been rather successful in controlling total health care expenditure during the 1980s. The share of GDP spent on health care puts Sweden very close to the OECD average.

Efficiency problems

Traditionally, the budget process in the county councils has determined how resources are allocated within the public health care system. Resources are allocated to production units based on their past use of input factors (labour, equipment, supplies, etc.). By closely controlling the use of staff, drugs and other material, the system has been successful in containing costs, but offered no information concerning efficiency. Management information is often inadequate. One incentive of this system of input reimbursement has been to spend the approved budget.[2] Furthermore, the distribution of resources across geographical areas shows variations unrelated to need. One explanation is that resource allocation has been provider-oriented and reflected provider interests instead of consumer needs.

The problem of management information and incentives might explain some of the deficiencies observed in the system. Long waiting lists were until recently observed for many surgical procedures. Studies and debates during the 1980s indicated efficiency losses and integration problems. Several studies have shown differences in productivity between public and private providers to the

Table 4.1 Judgements of the possibility of influencing service in different sectors

Sector	Average score (0–10)
Housing	5.3
Purchase of capital goods	6.5
Employment (work)	5.2
Day-nursery care	4.8
Education (mandatory school)	2.3
Health care	**4.4**
– Influencing care according to preferences	**3.8**
– Obtaining adequate care	**6.2**
– Own choice of doctor	**3.7**
– Change to another clinic or practice	**3.6**

Source: Peterson, Westholm and Blomberg (1987)

disadvantage of the former. Also the variations in productivity within the public sector are found to be significant.[3] The absence of competition was interpreted as one important contributor to these results. In the debate, abolition of the county councils was proposed, as well as a transfer of responsibility for health care to either the municipalities or implementing a social insurance system. However, different proposals for institutional changes of responsibility for health care have been rejected by a solid majority of politicians.

Consumer choice

Freedom of choice for the patient was limited due to the policy of geographical catchment areas. This strategy sought to improve the continuity of the provider–patient relationship. Especially in the primary health care sector, this strategy facilitated prevention measures for larger populations. At the same time the strategy gives little opportunity for patients to choose providers. Lack of consumer choice became a political issue in the discussions prior to the reforms. In 1985, the Government Committee on Power and Democracy in Sweden, basing its findings on 2000 interviews, showed that education, health care and child care received low scores regarding ability to influence service and to choose providers (Table 4.1).

As can been observed in the table, patients felt they had little opportunity to choose their providers, physician, or clinic. The study also showed that citizens considered the actual quality of care satisfactory.[4] But, combined with problems such as waiting lists and the

Table 4.2 Major reforms in the Swedish health care system

Reform	Year	Authority	Sector
Internal markets	1991–94	County councils	Health care
Family doctor reform	1994	Central government	Primary health care
Free establishment of doctors	1994	Central government	Private practitioners
Maximum waiting-time guarantee	1992	Central government/ County councils	Twelve procedures
The care of the elderly	1992	Central government/ County council homes	Nursing reform

need to cope with stagnant economic growth, the study helped precipitate discussions on the efficiency of the system that resulted in a series of reform proposals.

To sum up, the health care situation in Sweden has shifted from one of rapidly expanding resources to one of stagnation in resource growth. This change precipitated discussions on system efficiency and made it easier for new proposals to be considered. The present reforms must be attributed to the problems of efficiency and consumer choice.

REFORMS OF DELIVERY OF HEALTH SERVICES

The transfer of several functional areas in health care from mainly the central government to the county councils during the 1960s and 1970s was implemented incrementally. Developments during the 1990s show more radical changes in the structure of the system. Five major reforms were implemented during this period (Table 4.2).

This chapter focuses mainly on the purchaser/provider split within the county councils and the family doctor reform. These two reforms have thoroughly changed the structure of health care provision in the county councils.

The purchaser/provider split in the county councils

A common principle in the reforms has been to make politicians concentrate on the interest of citizens by separating the purchaser and provider roles within the county councils. The providers in these counties remain under public ownership, but politicians have decided not to be represented on the boards of hospitals and health centres. They therefore have less decision making power at the operational level. These changes aimed at introducing competition among providers and thereby increasing incentives to use available resources more efficiently. The political discussion preceding the implementation of the reforms raised criticism related to the domination of the provider perspective over the consumer perspective. As county council politicians act as both representatives for the providers (as owners) and the citizens, these roles were sometimes considered to be confused. With a strong influence from the medical profession, the politicians often took the view of the providers.

The movement toward market mechanisms in public health care can be summarized as encompassing the following attributes:

- collective purchasing units;
- freedom of choice for consumers;
- provider competition;
- contracts and performance-based reimbursement;
- provider autonomy.

In contrast to earlier changes affecting the organizational and financial structure of the county councils, individual county councils now develop their own management control systems. Changes in such systems during the 1960s and 1970s were designed and developed centrally by the Federation of County Councils.

The implementation of collective purchasing units has been structured differently. One group of county councils (Dalarna, Bohuslän) has decentralized the purchasing function to local units corresponding to primary health districts with populations of 6000–50,000. A second, intermediate approach established larger districts within the county councils, to act on behalf of consumers (Stockholm, Västerbotten). Finally, some county councils have established central agencies acting as a collective purchaser of health care for all citizens (Sörmland, Östergötland). The models separating purchaser and provider interests have been implemented gradually. Table 4.3 shows the county councils and specialties where a purchaser/provider split has been implemented.

The collective purchasing units usually receive their resources based on population characteristics (number of inhabitants, age, etc.). These resources are used to purchase health services from

Table 4.3 The implementation of internal markets in some county councils

Year	County council	Specialty	Purchaser/ Provider split	Prospective payment
1991	Dalarna	Somatic care	Local	Yes
1992	Stockholm	Some surgery	District	Yes (DRG)
	Dalarna	Psychiatry		No
	Örebro	Some surgery	Central	Yes (DRG)
1993	Stockholm	Somatic care		Yes (DRG)
	Bohuslän	All health care	Local	Yes (DRG)
	Östergötland	All health care	Central	No
	Örebro	Somatic care	Central	Yes (DRG)
	Sörmland	All health care	Central	Yes (DRG)
	Gävleborg	All health care	District	No
	Västerbotten	All health care	District	No

Note: DRG = Diagnosis Related Groups: a set of case types identifying patients with similar conditions and processes of care established for prospective payment systems.

providers within the county council, although contracts with external providers are also allowed.

The table indicates that by 1994 only eight of the 26 county councils had implemented models featuring a purchaser/provider split. These county councils represent 40 per cent of the total population in Sweden. This means that more than 50 per cent of the county councils' resources are still allocated by the traditional budget process. However, some of them use market mechanisms for a smaller segment of the health service. The table also shows that the purchase of health services was first implemented in the surgical specialties. Specialties with a higher degree of uncertainty about costs and outcome and where the output of the service is difficult to observe (psychiatry, geriatrics) were included later. The implementation of internal markets has also changed the way providers are reimbursed. The earlier budget process has been replaced by various performance-related reimbursement mechanisms (fee-for-service or fee-per-diagnosis). Such arrangements have been adopted slowly and applied where most appropriate.

The family doctor reform

The implementation of internal markets is decided regionally by individual county councils. In addition to these changes, central government decided to introduce the family doctor reform in 1994. Under this reform it became mandatory that all citizens should have the right to enrol with a family doctor. Previously, primary health care has been organized in public health centres with employed staff. Physicians received monthly salaries related to their qualifications and work schedule. Generally, patients were assigned to the health centres that were responsible for all citizens in their catchment area. As a result, the freedom to choose provider was limited until the beginning of the 1990s.

In larger cities there has also been a supply of private practitioners contracted by the county councils. These practitioners, especially private general practitioners, were also allowed to enter the system of family doctors and compete with public physicians. Under the new proposal, physicians were allowed to keep the out-of-pocket fees, a sum expected to contribute between 20–30 per cent of their income. In addition, they received a capitation payment, adjusted for age, for each patient on their list. These revenues were intended to cover the expenditures for service at the physician practice (such as nurses, supplies and facilities). Prescribed medicines are reimbursed separately by central government.

There is currently uncertainty about the family doctor reform as the Social Democratic government, which regained power in 1994, has decided to abolish it. However, several county councils have decided to continue with the reform, although others have returned to the previous system of public health centres and catchment areas.

The free establishment for private practitioners

Specialists in the private sector have received public payments, in addition to patient fees, through the social insurance system for many years. Since the mid-1980s they have needed authorization by the county council in order to receive payment from public sources. At the beginning of 1994 the non-socialist government gave all private practitioners the right to establish practices without the permission of the county council. The reform also had financial consequences for the county councils as the payments to the private practitioners reduced the resources for other activities in health care. During the summer and autumn of 1994 there was a significant increase in the establishment of private practitioners in the larger cities. The financial arrangement together with the right to establish a new practice made it difficult for the county councils to control utilization and costs. This reform has also been abolished by the Social Democratic government elected in 1994. However, those physicians who have already established their practice are guaranteed public reimbursement.

Maximum waiting time guarantee

In order to reduce the waiting time for certain treatments a national 'maximum waiting time guarantee' was introduced in 1992. This reform was a result of negotiations between the central government and the Federation of the County Councils. The guarantee states that a patient who is placed on a waiting list for one of 12 different diagnostic tests and treatments (coronary angiography, coronary artery bypass grafting, coronary angioplasty, hip and knee replacement, cataract surgery, inguinal hernia operation, cholecystectomy, operation for benign prostatic hyperplasia, operation for prolapse of the uterus, operation for incontinence, hearing-aid fitting) and cannot get his or her treatment within three months at the nearest hospital shall be offered the same medical care at another hospital. The alternative could be a hospital in the same or in another county or it could be a private hospital. The reform gave the county councils a strong incentive to increase productivity and admit patients to hospitals with shorter waiting time. With the guarantee, the patients' right to treatment has been specified in a formal way.

The care of the elderly reform

Another important reform that took place in 1992 was the care of the elderly reform. With this reform services for the elderly and disabled were reorganized with the municipalities being given full responsibility as well as the financial resources for these services. In practice, local nursing homes, comprising around 70 per cent of the total number of beds in somatic long-term care, were transferred from the county councils to the municipalities. From the same date the municipalities have also taken over the financial responsibility of patients who are fully treated and can be discharged from hospital.

There were two main reasons for this reform. The first is the expected increase in life expectancy with an escalating number of very old people. In order to obtain a better integration of different services for the elderly, it seemed rational to transfer the nursing homes to the municipalities, who already have the responsibility for social services. The second reason was that the organization of care and services for the elderly and disabled was not efficient regarding the division of responsibility between the county councils and the municipalities. The problem of so-called bed-blockers was considered to be an obstacle to increasing the number of treatments in the hospitals. The intention of the reform was to overcome this problem.

The basic principle for financing health care

Importantly, the current reforms do not change the way health care is financed. The principles of fairness and equity are strongly ingrained in the overall goals for Swedish health services. It is essential that factors such as age, income, sex, or place of residence do not become discriminatory. There is general political agreement that financing of health care should not be based on the ability to pay. Direct consumer charges are only nominal (£10–20) for a visit to a physician. Patient fees are still regulated by the central government which stipulates a maximum rate (£20). This gives the county councils some latitude to use fees as a rationing instrument. There is also a cost ceiling per patient per year of £160. In total, consumers' out-of-pocket expenses account for 10 per cent of total health care expenditures.

STRUCTURE/PROCESS EVALUATION OF THE REFORMS

Regulation and competition among health care providers

A major reason for separating the purchaser and provider functions in the county councils was to introduce competition among health service providers. Competition between providers has also been a key factor in the family doctor reform. An important aspect of the reforms was to break up the monopoly held by public providers. The market solutions being implemented do not involve the introduction of 'pure' markets into the system of provision. Rather, they create a kind of internal market or 'quasi-market', whereby tax financing of health care is maintained, but a form of managed competition is introduced into the system of care provision.

Market structure

For the market allocation of a service to be efficient, the market must be competitive. A number of conditions must be fulfilled, for example, many providers and purchasers, the possibility of free entry to and exit from the market, and so on. The market structure in the county councils differs in several respects from a conventional competitive market. Providers have been given considerable freedom to organize the production of health care. This autonomy is, however, constrained by regulations related to public ownership and associated objectives. For example, the decision to close down a hospital or a primary health care centre must be sanctioned by county council politicians. Major investments in facilities and equipment are controlled by regional political boards. Decisions about pure production issues such as the mix of labour and other inputs in the production process and investments below an upper limit have been decentralized to local managers.

However, politicians have resisted recommendations from hospital managers to lay off public employees during periods of recession. The shift toward free-standing providers is perceived by many hospital managers to be changeable and arbitrary. To a considerable extent, however, providers have become more free-standing and released from detailed regulation. A more professional leadership where managers are recruited from the private sector strengthens this process. Hospitals and other institutions are reimbursed by contracts or agreements with purchasing units. This process can be characterized as competitive tendering where mainly public providers compete among themselves.

On the purchasing side, two principal strategies can be observed in the reformed county councils. One alternative is based on a system of local purchasing units assisted by primary health care providers. These units represent around 5000–60,000 citizens and work in close cooperation with the primary health care physicians in the geographic area, for purchasing hospital and specialist services. Such models integrate purchasing with provision of primary health care. Accordingly a trade-off must be made between locally provided primary health services versus purchasing services from hospitals and specialists. Even if the purchasers locally have monopsony power, the hospitals are confronted by several purchasers. There is also the risk of a provider monopoly.

The second alternative involves the establishment of central agencies acting as one collective purchaser of the citizens' health services. The monopsony power of these units has been justified by the necessity to create large purchasers to deal with large providers, including hospitals. This also gives the purchasers a pure monopsony position toward local providers, for example, primary health care services.

It is obvious that the requirements for a competitive market are far from being met. Nevertheless, there is a departure from the earlier, vertically integrated model based on administrative coordination. The negotiation process itself has brought up issues concerning utilization patterns and quality which had not been explicitly considered in the previous budget process.

Competition among health care providers may refer to price as well as quality. The experience so far shows that prices are fixed administratively and decided centrally by the county councils. Negotiations in a marketplace involving several purchasers and providers have not been tested, even in subsectors characterized by multiple providers and purchasers, such as primary health care. Overall, competition has focused on accessibility and the quality of the service provided. This form of non-price competition has changed the incentives for providers to become more sensitive to customer satisfaction. Not surprisingly, incentives to treat patients have in some sectors increased total utilization and costs. To limit such behaviour, competition has been accompanied by various budgetary restrictions.

Entry to the market and private providers

The introduction of competition among public providers has also opened up the health care market for new private providers. Several of the county councils implementing internal markets have given private providers opportunities to tender for service contracts. In practice, the incumbent public provider usually receives the contract. Especially in the hospital sector, large investments and an uncertainty about the competitive neutrality of the public purchasers have made investors cautious about entering the market.

The family doctor reform also entitles private practitioners to enrol patients. The reform removed entry barriers to the primary health care market for new providers; in that market a large investment is not required. There was therefore free entry into the market, which is less costly than in the hospital sector. As shown in Table 4.4, the reform has increased the supply of private practitioners in the primary health care sector.[5]

Table 4.4   The supply of public and private family doctors in 1994

County council	Publicly employed physicians	Private physicians	Total	Physicians per 10,000 inhabitants (1994)	Physicians per 10,000 inhabitants (1993)
County councils with a high share of private family doctors					
U	83	56 (40.3%)	139	5.3	4.5
MM	78	45 (36.6%)	123	5.2	3.0
L	112	49 (30.4%)	161	5.5	—
AB	615	205 (25.0%)	820	4.9	4.0
N	95	29 (23.4%)	124	4.7	4.0
County councils with a low share of private family doctors					
X	145	11 (7.0%)	156	5.4	4.3
W	162	5 (3.0%)	167	5.8	5.0
S	145	4 (2.7%)	149	5.2	4.1
Y	126	2 (1.6%)	128	4.9	4.5
G	85	1 (1.2%)	86	4.8	4.5

Key: U   = Västmanland   X = Gävleborg
       MM = Malmö kommun   W = Dalarna
       L   = Kristianstad   S = Värmland
       AB = Stockholm   Y = Västernorrland
       N   = Halland   G = Kronoberg
Source: Rehnberg and Garpenby (1995)

The entry of new providers has improved the physician to population ratio. There is now no shortage of primary health care physicians in the rural areas. Most of the new family doctors come from the private sector and occupational health service. There are also some publicly employed physicians who have started their own practices.

Efficiency requires that there should be the possibility of exit in the market, that is, providers should face the risk of bankruptcy. One major problem for the county councils with the family doctor reform concerns those publicly employed primary care physicians who did not sign up enough patients in the enrolment process. Their status as employees implies that they could not be laid off even if they fail to meet the enrolment quota. This has been a controversial issue which led to a physicians' strike in the spring of 1994. The Federation of County Councils and the Swedish Medical Association still disagree about how to handle publicly employed physicians who fail to enrol sufficient patients. Hence, the county councils are faced with a situation of free entry for private practitioners but no exit for publicly employed family physicians. To solve this problem new forms of associations for public doctors will probably be required.

Contractual relationships

The interaction between the consumer and the provider side of the county councils takes place in an internal or a quasi-market. The demand side consists of two actors, purchasing units and individual consumers. The purchasing units act as agents for the consumer or the citizens and sign the contracts on the demand side. Individual consumers influence resource allocation by their choice of providers.

Purchasing units receive their revenues on a capitation basis and draw up service contracts with public and private providers. The purchasers should strive to maximize the health status of the population within their budgets. To what extent this purpose is met or whether purchasers pursue their own agenda is hard to judge. As monopoly purchasers they have no clear incentives to act in the interests of the population. Over time, the change in the politicians' role from acting in the interests of both consumers and providers to acting as pure purchasing agents for citizens may lead to a clearer focus on the consumer interests.

Bilateral monopoly and informational advantage

Under the earlier planning model, county councils built hospitals, nursing homes and primary health care centres within a defined catchment area. The location of facilities implied a monopoly position for several providers. This presents difficulties in creating competition between providers. The problem with dominant providers is greatest in the hospital sector where, apart from the three largest cities, most cities have only one hospital. Furthermore, given that Sweden is a sparsely populated country, it is not obvious that a competitive market with a larger number of providers would be more allocatively efficient since advantages of large-scale production probably exist in the hospital sector.

This could be solved by an increasing use of distant providers and by exposing incumbent providers to competition from potential providers. Several polls show that citizens are reluctant to travel long distances to receive health services. However, in regions where several county councils agree on a free choice of providers across boundaries, the actual behaviour of patients shows changes in the consumption pattern. In the case of natural monopolies, purchasers have the possibility to use the potential for competition, that is the opportunity for new providers to enter the market. Yet such an arrangement presents investment problems and an uncertainty among potential new providers about the neutrality of public purchasers when deciding between public and private providers in the bargaining process.

Access to information also affects the efficiency of internal markets. A condition for a market relationship is that both purchaser and provider have accurate information about costs, prices, quality and other attributes of the services available. Given a more autonomous position, competing providers would become reluctant to share all information about costs and resources needed. Providers might engage in opportunistic behaviour, that is where one party realizes gains by concealing information, and thereby imposing costs on the other party. There are examples on both the purchasing and provision side where information which was earlier public has now become confidential.

In general, providers have better access to information than purchasers. Management control systems are naturally controlled by the providers. Also, the most experienced managers have been recruited to run larger hospitals. In the initial stage of introducing market mechanisms, providers are much better prepared for negotiation and bargaining. Along with the establishment of separate purchasing units, staff with competence in accounting and management as well as in epidemiology and social medicine are recruited. Informational asymmetry may diminish over time, and purchasers in some county councils claim they are in a better position to bargain with providers than they were in the previous budgetary process.

Contract structure

In the reform process, the traditional allocation of resources is being replaced by contractual relationships between purchasers and providers. The nature and level of services will be specified in the contracts together with the reimbursement principle. There are two major forms of contracts.

First, there are block contracts where the purchaser pays a yearly sum in return for access to a defined range of services. The capacity for a specific service is defined with this type of contractual agreement. Block contracts are primarily found in medical specialties (psychiatry, geriatrics) where the output is difficult to verify. A problem with this arrangement is that contracts are incomplete, which opens up the possibility for opportunistic behaviour. With major information asymmetry in these specialties, both the provider and purchaser, but especially the purchaser, are faced with risk. The purchaser has limited opportunities to monitor output and the outcome of services delivered. The provider also risks unexpected increases in costs due to uncertain utilization patterns.

One important attribute in these contracts is performance targets, such as maximum waiting list targets, which entitle the patient to treatment within a specified time. This part of the contract has been judged to have a significant influence on provider behaviour. Earlier waiting times, mainly for surgical procedures (which sometimes were measured in years), have almost disappeared or been reduced to months.

Second, there are performance-related contracts which are mainly found in surgical specialties and internal medicine where output is observable and forms the basis of reimbursement. Some county councils are using the Diagnosis Related Groups (DRG) classification, whereas others use measures such as admissions and visits. Additional resources are allocated separately for units with a complex case-mix and commitments such as education and research. These contracts are sometimes combined with a ceiling for total utilization intended to control costs. Prices are generally based on average costs, but pricing based on marginal costs is used above a certain level of activity. The problems associated with performance-related contracts include price uncertainty (as no market price exists) and the incentive for overutilization of services.

The experience so far is that purchasers are more successful at controlling costs for units they have signed contracts with which include figures about a maximum utilization or expenditure level. Also providers who are interested in establishing a long-run commitment with purchasers would not try to use the reimbursement system to achieve short-term increases in revenues.

THE EFFECTS AND RESULTS OF THE REFORMS

Freedom of choice and consumer sovereignty

The reforms have substantially increased the individual's opportunities to choose providers. Two alternatives have been considered concerning how the choice of providers can be arranged. The first alternative is to design reimbursement so that the money directly follows the patient. This voucher-like arrangement would force providers to profile themselves to attract patients. The second alternative would be to use patient choice as a guidance system in the negotiations between purchasing units and providers. Resources to health services would continue to be allocated mainly via collective decisions, but patients, by their choice of provider, would show their preferences.

The implementation of the family doctor reform gave patients a defined right to choose a provider in primary health care. An increased opportunity to choose providers is also central to several of the internal market models introduced by the county councils. In a number of county councils patients can choose among public and private providers and among physicians as well as hospital clinics. The choice is not completely free but is limited by the contracts signed by purchasing units. Agreements have been signed between some county councils concerning the right of patients to choose providers across boundaries.

Overall, the patient's choice of providers, limited by a defined supply of providers, as specified in contracts signed with purchasing units, has been the most powerful means to change provider behaviour. A significant improvement in accessibility and customer service is reported from many county councils. The effects on total resource allocation are, however, limited. About 2–5 per cent of total resources are reportedly redistributed because of consumer choice.

In all county council models with a purchaser/provider split, patients have been given a great deal of freedom to choose providers. This has given rise to a coordination problem on the demand side that has to be solved. Providers are faced with formal contracts signed by an agent on behalf of the citizens and, at the same time, by individual choices. These two signals are not always concurrent. Consumers may choose other providers or consume a higher volume of health services than specified in the contracts. At present, no strategy deals sufficiently with the different signals sent to providers.

Equity and equal access to health care

The equity principle has been a major argument for maintaining public financing of health care. In that respect, the introduction of internal markets does not change the opportunities for receiving care. Universal insurance coverage and low patient fees guarantee

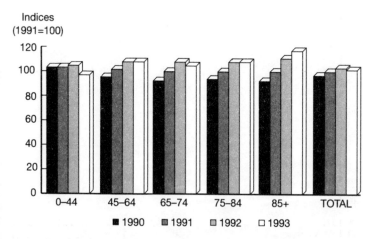

Indices
(1991=100)

■ 1990   ▨ 1991   ▨ 1992   □ 1993

Figure 4.2 Treated patients per age-group in the Stockholm County Council, 1990–93
Source: Paulsson (1994)

equal access to care. However, it has been argued that the equity principle could be violated in an internal market. As the purchasing units are pressured to use resources as efficiently as possible, they would concentrate on acute care where the treatment outcomes are observable. This might be at the expense of care for chronic psychiatric and geriatric patients. Deficiencies in the reimbursement system to compensate providers for severe cases might reinforce such discrimination.

The utilization of health care resources across age-groups has sometimes been used as a measure of how needs are met. During the last 20 years there has been a radical shift in health care consumption from the younger and middle-aged groups to the elderly. The very old have increased their consumption both in absolute and relative terms.[6] As the productivity increase in some county councils to a large extent is explained by an increase in production (and not by an decrease in costs), it is interesting to study which age group has benefited from this increase.

Figure 4.2 shows that the oldest age-group has increased their utilization most.[7] This is not surprising since most patients on the earlier waiting lists were the elderly. Furthermore, these figures give no support to the argument that internal markets discriminate against the elderly.

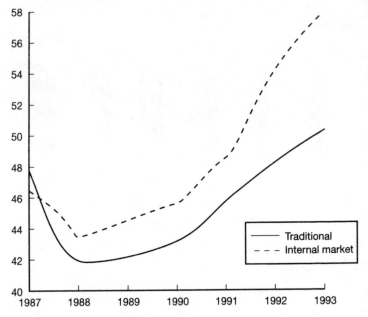

Figure 4.3 Admissions per beds, department of surgery, 1987–93
Source: The Federation of the County Councils (1995)

Efficiency

To what extent the introduction of competition has changed the behaviour of providers is too early to define. Previous behaviour, where public providers used long waiting lists to gain more resources in the budget process, has disappeared. Under a reimbursement system based on performance, providers must increase their workload to attract more resources. An increase in productivity has been observed in most county councils, in particular in the surgical specialties. In Figures 4.3 and 4.4, this development is shown for the eight county councils which have implemented some kind of internal market, compared with the county councils using the traditional budget process.[8]

According to the figures, an overall increase in productivity can be observed in the early 1990s. However, it is clear that this trend is stronger in the group of county councils using internal market systems. The productivity growth for in-patient care can be explained by either a reduction of resources (beds) and/or by an increase in performance (admissions/operations). The traditional

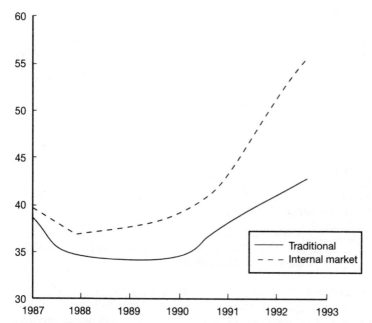

Figure 4.4 Surgical operations per bed (in-patient), 1987–93
Source: The Federation of the County Councils (various years)

county councils have mainly achieved a higher productivity by reducing the number of beds, whereas the county councils using internal markets have also improved their performance. For specialties such as internal medicine and psychiatry, the differences between the two groups do not seem to be of the same magnitude. However, the incentive for providers to generate revenues could result in overtreatment or cost-shifting (e.g. out-patient care or long-term care).

Also, several case studies show a drop in the utilization of ancillary services within hospitals and a greater awareness among staff concerning the financial situation of their provider units. Interview studies indicate that physicians pay more attention to costs in their practice than before. From the consumer perspective, improved accessibility and service has been reported.

Administrative costs

A central issue regarding contractual relationships is the volume of administrative activity. Administrative costs accompany both

Table 4.5   Administrative costs as a percentage of total expenditures for different third party payers

Health care system	Share of total expenditures (per cent)
Sweden	
County councils: Stockholm	4–5
Dalarna	3.0
Social insurance (private physicians)	1.5
United States	
Medicare	2.1
Medicaid	3.2–11.8
HMO	2.5–7.0
Private insurance	
– business	5.5–40
– individual	40

Sources: Rehnberg (1993) and Thorpe (1992)

integrated systems and contract relationships between independent buyers and sellers. It should also be noted that to focus exclusively on lowering the level of administrative costs can generate problems in controlling utilization and thus total costs. For example, the Swedish social insurance system costs little to run but has had difficulty controlling use by private practitioners. Generally, insurance systems with individual enrolment and individual premiums have higher administrative costs (Table 4.5).[9]

Table 4.5 shows that monopoly insurers experience lower administrative costs. The share of administrative costs has not increased substantially with the introduction of internal markets in Sweden. Since the reforms do not change the universal coverage of the insured and do not include individual enrolment with individual risk evaluation, it is unlikely that administrative costs will increase drastically. However, experience suggests that *ex ante* administrative costs, that is those which precede production, are greater in agreements with external providers. On the other hand, *ex post* costs, that is costs of control and evaluation, are greater in integrated systems. County councils with multiple purchasing units fear the expansion of administrative activities. One way to reduce those costs would be through cooperation among small local units.

The administrative costs on the provider side have not been estimated. As the administrative costs by the providers are included in the reimbursement payment to the hospitals and the clinics, an increase in administrative measures is likely to reduce other activities at the clinics. Given the reported increase in productivity, it is unlikely that the administrative costs have increased dramatically. Given the present results there are no indications of major increases in administrative costs on either the purchaser or the provider sides.[10]

CONCLUSION

The implementation of internal markets in public health care is at an early stage and it is too soon to make judgements about the long-term consequences in terms of efficiency and equity. In the discussion of market-oriented reforms, a number of concepts have been used to analyse the market structure. As has been shown in this chapter, internal markets in health care differ in several respects from a conventional competitive market.

Several characteristics of a competitive market are absent in the internal market model. The shift towards market mechanisms concerns mainly the use of financial incentives through new ways of reimbursing providers. Prices are regulated and controlled at the central level in most county councils. The second change of importance is the increased freedom for consumers to choose providers. This voucher-like arrangement is reported to have had a major impact on the providers' behaviour. Also the stipulation in contracts about maximum waiting times for specific procedures has given the consumer a stronger position. Improved accessibility and reduced waiting lists are observed.

Regarding the competitiveness of the market, there are still several regulations. The mechanisms to enter and exit the market are not developed. In general, the market structure can be regarded as involving regulated competition between public providers.

The market-oriented reforms in health care have changed the principles for resource allocation. Analyses have still to be carried out in order to identify which mechanisms contribute to changes in utilization and efficiency. Contrary to the interpretation that higher productivity, reductions in waiting lists and so on can be related solely to the implementation of internal markets, similar trends are sometimes reported from county councils relying on the traditional planning models.

However, the experience so far is that these effects are stronger in county councils using internal markets for resource allocation. On the other hand, these county councils seem to have bigger problems in terms of cost containment. The experience is also that the purchase of health services was first implemented in the surgical specialties. Specialties with a higher degree of uncertainty about costs and outcome and where the output of the service is difficult to observe were included later.

The structure of the internal markets is also changing over time. As in any market, regulations and other arrangements between consumers and producers is a learning process where each party gains experience upon the nature of the market that will evolve in the future.

NOTES

1   The Federation of the County Councils (various years) *Statistisk årsbok för landsting (Statistical Yearbook)*. Stockholm: Landstingsförbundet.
2   B. Jönsson and C. Rehnberg (1987) *Effektivare sjukvård (More Efficient Medical Care)*. Stockholm: Norstedts.
3   B. Lindgren and P. Roos (1985) *Produktions- kostnads- och produktivitetsutveckling inom offentligt bedriven hälso- och sjukvård 1960–1980 (Production, Cost and Productivity Growth in Public Health Care 1960–1980)*. Stockholm: DsFi 1983: 3.
4   O. Peterson, A. Westholm and G. Blomberg (1987) *Medborgarnas makt (The power of the citizens)*. Stockholm: Carlsson Bokförlag.
5   C. Rehnberg and P. Garpenby (1995) *Privata aktörer i Svensk sjukvård (Private Actors in the Swedish Health Care System)*. Stockholm: SNS.
6   U.G. Gerdtham (1993) The impact of ageing on health care expenditure in Sweden. *Health Policy*, 24: 1–11.
7   E. Paulsson (1994) *Fyra kirurgiska specialiteter i Stockholmsmodellen (Four surgical specialties in the Stockholm-model)*. Uppsala: Uppsala University.
8   The Federation of the County Councils (various years) *Statistisk årsbok för landsting (Statistical Yearbook)*. Stockholm: Landstingsförbundet.
9   K.E. Thorpe (1992) Inside the black box of administrative costs. *Health Affairs*, 11: 41–55; C. Rehnberg (1993) *Administrationskostnader inom hälso- och sjukvården (Administrative Costs in Health Care)*. Bilaga I in SOU 1993: 38 Hälso- och sjukvården i framtiden - Tre modeller. Stockholm: Socialdepartementet.
10 C. Rehnberg, (1993) *Administrationskostnader inom hälso- och sjukvården (Administrative Costs in Health Care)*. Bilaga I in SOU 1993: 38 Hälso- och sjukvården i framtiden - Tre modeller. Stockholm: Socialdepartementet.

5

THE NETHERLANDS
Wynand van de Ven

INTRODUCTION

Health care reforms in the Netherlands are inspired by
Enthoven's Consumer-Choice Health Plan and are based on the
report of the Dekker Committee which was published in 1987.[1]
The two key elements of the proposed system are compulsory
health insurance for the whole population and regulated competition. The reforms can be characterized as a transition from
government regulated cartels to government regulated competition among insurers as well as providers of care. Competing
insurers are supposed to contract selectively with competing
providers of care. Insurers therefore function as third-party purchasers of care. Since 1989 a step by step implementation of the
reforms has taken place. A number of major changes have
occurred but new problems have emerged.

In this chapter we will describe the main lines of the reforms and
sketch the progress made so far; what has and has not been realized
and what new problems arose. What can other countries learn from
the experience of health care reform in the Netherlands? We will
also indicate how in 1995 the reform proposals were adjusted by the
government that came into office in 1994. A major element of the
new government's proposal is the continuation of the Dekker
reforms only as far as non-catastrophic risks are concerned (e.g.
hospital care, physician services, drugs). Consequently the government also changed the implementation path of the reforms. Finally
we will discuss the most likely developments in the Dutch health
care reforms for the future.

HEALTH CARE REFORMS IN THE NETHERLANDS

Why such radical reforms?

In a letter to Parliament in March 1988 the Dutch government mentioned the following four reasons for reforming the health care system.[2] First, the uncoordinated financing structure for health care and social welfare (homes for the aged, family assistance programmes and social work) impedes cost-effective substitution of care. Closely interrelated forms of health care delivery are frequently artificially separated by multiple financing mechanisms and complex regulations.

Second, the Dutch health care system is characterized by a lack of incentives for efficiency. The financing system is such that in many cases economic and efficient behaviour is financially punished, while non-economic and inefficient behaviour is financially rewarded. Therefore, changing the present financing system is a necessary condition for improving efficiency in health care.

Third, according to government, the very detailed regulation of capacity planning in health care has turned out to be unworkable. This failure is due to the complexity of the planning process, the many parties involved, their conflicting interests, and the lack of clarity of regulation. A major problem appears to be the relationship between planning and financing. A crucial question is whether planning should precede financing or whether planning should follow financing decisions. In the present system, planning and financing decisions are made separately, causing many problems. None of the parties involved is fully responsible for the consequences of their decisions.

Fourth, there are several problems with the present Dutch health insurance system. All employees (and their families) earning an annual wage below 60,000 guilders (which is equivalent to US$ 35,000 at the 1995 exchange rate) are compulsorily insured by one of the 20 sickness funds. This also holds true after retirement. Except for a limited group of civil servants who have their own mandatory scheme, the remainder of the population (about 34 per cent), consisting mainly of self-employed and higher income groups, can voluntarily buy private health insurance. They are able to choose among one of the 50 competing private health insurers operating in the Netherlands. In addition, there is a compulsory national health insurance scheme (Algemene Wet Bijzondere Ziektekosten) providing coverage for the whole population against catastrophic risks, such as hospital care exceeding one year, long-term nursing home care, and long-term institutional care for mentally and physically handicapped persons. Without going into details, the many problems in the Dutch health insurance system are related to the existence of different insurance schemes with different premium structures, and the effects of an unregulated competitive market for private health insurance.[3]

The above four arguments for reform were set out in 1988 by the then centre–right coalition cabinet. Two years later the new cabinet, a centre–left coalition, endorsed these arguments, particularly stressing the failure of detailed government regulation of volume, prices and productive capacity. According to the government the major cause of this failure was that only government was responsible for cost containment. All other parties – providers, insurers and patients – could oppose government regulation without committing themselves in any way. The government seriously doubted that, in a system in which government was the only controlling factor, in the long run cost could be maintained without jeopardizing the quality of care. Therefore, from the government's point of view, a major purpose of the proposed reform was to share responsibility for cost containment in health care with the other parties, that is the providers, the insurers and the population.

Reform proposal

In 1988 the Dutch government and parliament decided to radically reform the health care system. The aim of the reform is to achieve a balance between accessibility ('equity') and market oriented financial incentives ('efficiency'). In 1990 the main lines of the reform proposal were also accepted by the then new government and the reforms became known as Plan-Simons, after the State Secretary for Health, Hans Simons.[4] Although the 1988 reforms are the same as those proposed in 1990, the vocabulary is different, reflecting Simons's social democratic background. Key words in the 1988 proposal of the then centre–right coalition cabinet were competition, market and incentives. In the 1990 proposal of the centre–left coalition cabinet these key words were replaced by terms like shared responsibility between parties, consumer choice and decentralization. Nevertheless, the main lines of Plan-Simons (1990) are the same as those of Plan-Dekker (1987).

The proposed system can be best characterized as a compulsory health insurance for the whole population, based on regulated competition. Direct government control over prices and productive capacities will have to make way for regulated competition among insurers and health care providers. Price cartels and regional cartels that have originated as the result of anti-competitive government regulation and self-regulation will be broken down. The benefits package of the compulsory health insurance will be very comprehensive and will consist of nearly all non-catastrophic risks (hospital care, physician services, drugs, physiotherapy and some dental care), catastrophic risks (nursing home care, long-term institutional care for mentally and physically handicapped persons) and health care related social welfare (old people's homes). Besides the compulsory health insurance, people are free to buy voluntary supplementary health insurance.

According to the government's proposal, all individuals will receive a subsidy to help them buy their *compulsory* health insurance from one of the competing insurers. The premium of the voluntary supplementary insurance will not be subsidized or regulated. The subsidy will come from a Central Fund which will be formed from mandatory incomes-related premiums, to be paid to the tax collector. From the Central Fund the subsidy will go directly to the qualified insurer chosen by the insured. Qualified insurers are not allowed to refuse any insured in their working area and have to obey other pro-competitive regulation. The maximum contract period is two years. At least once every two years the consumer may choose another insurer. The subsidy for each individual is independent of the chosen insurer and will be equal to the expected per capita health care costs within the risk group to which the insured person belongs, less a fixed amount which is the same for all individuals. The deficit created by this fixed amount is met by a flat rate premium to be paid by the insured person directly to the insurer of his or her choice.

An insurer is obliged to quote the same flat rate premium to all insured people who choose the same insurance contract. The insurers' revenues consist of the risk-adjusted per capita payments from the Central Fund, supplemented by the flat rate premiums to be paid by insured people. The difference between the actual costs and the risk-adjusted payment will not be the same for all insurers and will be reflected in the flat rate premium that the competing insurers quote. This creates an incentive for insurers to be efficient.

The insurers are expected to function as an intermediary between the consumer and the provider of care. To a great extent, insurers and providers will be free to negotiate the contractual terms. Insurers will be allowed to selectively contract with providers and to offer different insurance contracts, as long as they provide coverage for all the types of care as described by law. Consumers will be free to choose among different insurers, picking the modality of the standardized benefits package they like the most. Some people will prefer a traditional health insurance contract with free choice of provider, while others may prefer a limited provider plan with a lower premium. Furthermore the premium paid will reflect the efficiency and cost-generating behaviour of the contracted health care providers. In this way it is expected that a situation will arise in which:

- insured people are rewarded for choosing efficient insurers and choosing cost-effective providers of care;
- providers are rewarded for effective and efficient provision of care;
- insurers, acting as intermediaries between insured people and contracted providers, are stimulated to contract efficient providers and to do market research to find out about the consumers' preferences.

What has and has not been realized?

According to the 1988 proposal the reform should have been implemented by the end of 1992. The 1990 proposal extended the implementation period by three years although this time schedule appeared to be too optimistic. When we look at the two key elements of the proposed reform, that is compulsory health insurance for all and regulated competition, we conclude that neither is implemented. Nevertheless, the following steps toward a market-oriented health care have been realized.

From 1993 sickness funds received a partially risk-adjusted capitation payment from the Central Fund for most of the non-catastrophic risks (hospital care, physician services, drugs, physiotherapy and some dental care). In addition, each insured person has to pay a flat rate premium to his or her sickness fund. In 1995 the flat rate premium was about 10 per cent of total health expenditures. Each sickness fund is free to determine its own flat rate premium. In effect, the main lines of the proposed financing system have been introduced in the sickness fund sector which covers 62 per cent of the population. This implies a radical change. During the period 1941–91 all sickness funds received a full reimbursement of all their medical expenditures. Therefore sickness funds are now in a transition from administrative bodies to risk-bearing enterprises.

From 1994 sickness funds had the option to contract selectively with physicians and pharmacists. This too implies a radical change. From 1941 sickness funds had the legal obligation to contract with each provider in their working area who wanted a contract.

From 1992 sickness funds and private health insurers were allowed to negotiate lower fees with providers than officially approved fees. During the period 1982–92 it was an economic offence to charge higher or lower fees than those officially approved.

Furthermore, from 1992 sickness funds were permitted to extend their regional working area and to gain members in other parts of the country. This was practically impossible to do in the past because the required permission was usually not given. Now almost all sickness funds are working nationwide.

Also, from 1992 several private health insurance companies established a new sickness fund organization. This implies an open entry to the sickness fund market. During the period 1941–91 no new sickness funds were established except by mergers of existing funds. From 1992 sickness fund members had the option to choose another sickness fund at least once every two years. Each sickness fund has to accept each applicant who is eligible for insurance. This means potential competition among sickness funds based on the flat rate premium, quality, the contracted providers, service, responsiveness, and reputation.

Finally, from 1992 general practitioners (GPs) were free to open a practice wherever they wanted. Until 1992 GPs needed a licence from the municipality to start a practice.

Looking at the above changes in legislation we may conclude that they are important steps towards a market-oriented health care system and that these steps can be expected to fundamentally change the functioning and organization of Dutch health care. The point of no return towards regulated competition on both the insurance and the provider market for non-catastrophic risks has been passed.

What effects?

For several reasons it is much too early for a full evaluation of the reforms so far. First, major effects of changes in legislation cannot be expected at short notice. Second, sickness fund organizations, which play a key role in the reform process, have a 50 year history as regional administrative bodies and cannot be expected to become entrepreneurial, risk-bearing and consumer-oriented organizations overnight. Third, because of the imperfection of the risk-adjusted capitation payments, sickness funds are responsible for only 3 per cent of the differences between their actual expenditures and the normative expenditure level on which the risk-adjusted capitation payments are based. The remaining 97 per cent of their expenses is still reimbursed retrospectively. Therefore the sickness funds' incentive for efficiency and stimulating managed care is still virtually non-existent. Fourth, despite the above mentioned changes, a substantial part of the old regulatory regime is still in force, for example, with respect to hospital budgeting and hospital planning. This hinders the full development of the reforms.

Although it is too early for a complete evaluation, the following effects of the reforms are worth mentioning. As the result of only the discussion about a more market-oriented health care system, we see a huge increase during the early 1990s in the activities concerning quality improvement and quality assurance. Probably the main driving force for all these quality improving activities is the idea that quality of care will be the major issue in a competitive health care system. From the early 1990s we see increasing investments in cost-accounting systems by hospitals and other health care institutions. Knowledge about the nature and real costs of the different services is necessary in a more competitive market. It prevents providers of care from selling products below costs and it enables insurers to be prudent buyers of care and to make the appropriate trade-off between products that are substitutes for each other.

Since the early 1990s we see a total reorganization of the internal structure of sickness funds. Administration-oriented chief executives who go into early retirement are replaced by entrepreneurial, market-oriented managers. The service to their members is being improved, such as better opening hours and mobile offices. From the early 1990s we see several innovative activities. For example, sickness funds have broken the price cartel of providers of some medical devices. Subsequently, prices went down by a quarter to a third. Insurers are developing mail order firms as an alternative distribution method of pharmaceuticals. All kinds of electronic data interchange (EDI) projects are being developed, aimed at improved cooperation among providers and a more efficient cooperation between providers and insurers.

Reasons for slow progress

Although the implementation of the reforms is far behind schedule, from an historic point of view radical changes have been realized within a relatively short period of time. Take, for example, the abolition of the contract obligation for sickness funds. During the first decades of this century there has been conflict between sickness funds and physicians about whether or not sickness funds should have the option to contract selectively with physicians. Ultimately the physicians won this conflict and from 1941 until 1991 sickness funds had the legal obligation to enter into a uniform contract with each physician established in their working area. Though creating the opportunity for selective contracting is not the same as putting it into practice, it certainly is a fundamental change from an historic point of view.

Those who are familiar with the history of the Dutch health care policy would probably have foreseen that the government's time schedule was far too optimistic. On the other hand, if the government had announced a more realistic time schedule, say 10 to 15 years, probably nothing would have changed. As discussed earlier, the credible threat of competition has generated an enormous change in conduct of all parties involved.

At least four reasons can be mentioned for the slow progress of the reforms. First, there has been resistance from interest groups who are powerful lobbies. Dutch health policy is characterized by a diffuse decision making structure without a clear-cut centre of power. Hence, the government cannot impose changes without the consent of major interest groups, such as the organizations of physicians, health insurers, employers and employees.[5] The employers opposed Plan-Simons because they were afraid that the government would pay more attention to the compulsory health insurance with a broad benefits package. This would increase total health care costs (because of moral hazard), rather than promote cost containment and improve efficiency. Because the premium is partly paid by the employers, increases in health expenditures would increase their labour costs and therefore affect their competitive position in the world market. The insurers opposed Plan-Simons because they strongly opposed a system of risk-adjusted capitation payments from the Central Fund and other government regulation that reduces their entrepreneurial freedom. The physicians opposed Plan-Simons because they found the description of the benefits package too general, leaving too much room for competition among providers of care.

A second reason for the slow progress of the reform is that the chosen implementation strategy triggered growing political opposition. From a political point of view the two key elements of the reforms are well balanced. The compulsory health insurance is attractive for those on the left; regulated competition is attractive for those on the right. This political balance of the reform proposal explains why both a centre–right and a centre–left coalition cabinet supported the proposal. However, because of the complexity of the reforms, they have to be implemented step by step, but this introduces a new complexity. In order to be politically acceptable, each step has to be as balanced as the whole reform proposal. According to the perception of the politicians this was not the case. The political right, supported by the employers, strongly opposed some steps because in their opinion more emphasis was put on the implementation of the compulsory health insurance than on cost containment efforts. Another political problem is that the introduction of a compulsory health insurance for the whole population is likely to generate negative income-redistribution effects for relatively young and healthy middle-class people with private health insurance because they will have to subsidize the poor and the unhealthy by paying an income-related premium instead of the present, considerably lower risk-related premium.[6]

Third, there is no urgent need for quick reform. In a sense the reorganization of the health care system is aimed at anticipating the problems of the next century: advances in medical technology, an ageing population, and an expected increase of the share of gross national product going to health care. From a macro economic point of view a step by step reform of the health care system can be afforded.

Fourth, the technical complexity of the reforms is very high and has seriously been underestimated. Several problems relate to the process of implementation, such as the coordination of overlapping and sometimes inconsistent new and old regulations, the avoidance of substantial negative wealth effects for parts of the population, and the fine tuning with complex EU regulations. Another important problem concerns the content and the appropriate definition of the benefits that should be covered by the compulsory insurance. In addition, the problem of maintaining a workable competitive health care system has to be addressed, which requires the development and enforcement of an effective anti-cartel policy in health care.[7] Probably the most vexing problem, however, is related to the proposed role of the insurer as a third-party purchaser of health care on behalf of the consumer. This problem is how to prevent cream skimming (or preferred risk selection) in a competitive health insurance market where insurers receive a risk-adjusted capitation payment.[8]

HEALTH CARE REFORMS IN THE NETHERLANDS: AFTER 1994

Although the then government had announced several major steps to be taken in 1993 and 1994 in order to further implement the proposed reform, in reality the implementation process in these years virtually ceased. At that time there was much confusion as to whether Plan-Simons was dead or not. And if it was dead, what then should be the alternative? In May 1995 the new government announced its health care policy for the coming years.[9]

The major change that the new coalition cabinet announced was that within the compulsory health insurance system there should be *two* regulatory regimes, and no longer *one* regulatory regime as in Plan-Dekker and Plan-Simons. The new government stated that it would continue the Dekker–Simons type of reform only for the non-catastrophic risks (like hospital care, physician services, drugs and physiotherapy). For the catastrophic risks (like nursing home care, and long-term institutional care for mentally and physically handicapped persons) and health care related social welfare (old people's homes) there will be direct government regulation with respect to planning, budgeting and prices. For these types of care there will be no role for competing risk-bearing insurers. In order to contain costs and improve efficiency in that sector, the government announced an independent system of indication setting and the introduction of a system of personal budgets for certain categories of patients, so that these patients can buy their care out of their own budget. So the question whether Plan-Dekker–Simons is dead or not, can be answered: yes, as far as the catastrophic risks are concerned; no, as far as the non-catastrophic risks are concerned.

With respect to the non-catastrophic risks, the dominant regulatory regime will be the Dekker model of regulated competition among insurers as well as among providers of care. The government announced plans to deregulate hospital planning, although for the time being the government will continue to bear the responsibility with respect to large scale investments related to hospital building. But for the remainder the government holds the view that competing risk-bearing insurers are, more than government, able to contain costs and improve efficiency, provided that there is enough competition. For this reason, the government announced an active and critical competition or anti-trust policy in health care. In order to increase the insurers' financial incentive to be a prudent buyer of health care for their members, the government aims to increase the financial responsibility of insurers and sickness funds.

Consequently the government will also increase the insurers' tools for improving efficiency by taking away the existing legal regulation concerning hospital budgeting. In addition the government decided to implement the proposals of the Biesheuvel committee.[10] This committee, chaired by former Prime Minister Biesheuvel, advised the government to promote the participation of specialists in the management structure of hospitals, to stimulate the integration of specialists and hospitals into one organization, and to replace the fee-for-service payment system by a remuneration system with fewer incentives to stimulate production. With respect to the remuneration of general practitioners (GPs), the Biesheuvel committee advised the introduction of a flexible system of bonuses, related to efficiency and other performance indicators.

Convergence: The new implementation path

As a consequence of the decision to have two regulatory regimes instead of one, within the compulsory health insurance system, the government also had to choose another implementation path. During the last seven years the implementation path of the reform was as follows:

- all non-catastrophic risks (to be included in the compulsory health insurance) should be transferred from the sickness fund insurance and the private health insurance to the AWBZ, which was intended to become the 'carrier' of the reformed health insurance system;
- the regulatory regime of the AWBZ should be reformed;
- ultimately all different regulatory regimes for sickness fund insurance and private health insurance would be abolished.

Sickness fund organizations and private health insurance companies should all become 'care insurers' with the same rights and duties.

Because the new government decided to have two strictly separated regulatory regimes for the catastrophic and the non-catastrophic risks, it no longer makes sense to continue the process of transferring non-catastrophic risks to the AWBZ. Instead the government proposed to restrict the AWBZ to only the catastrophic risks, and to transfer all non-catastrophic risks that are currently covered under the AWBZ (e.g. prescription drugs) to the sickness funds and private health insurance. In addition the government announced a convergence of sickness fund and private health insurance. That is, for the time being the distinction between sickness fund insurance and private health insurance will be maintained, but over time the differences between these two types of insurance will disappear.

In the sickness fund sector the government proposed to drastically increase the financial risk for the sickness funds. In 1995 the sickness funds received risk-adjusted capitation payments based on age, gender, region and disability. Currently it is a partial capitation system in the sense that the sickness funds are responsible for only about 3 per cent of the difference between their actual expenses and the predicted expenses based on age, gender, region and disability. The remaining 97 per cent is retrospectively reimbursed. The new government announced that the 3 per cent figure will be increased to 100 per cent by the year 1998 (except for the fixed hospital costs).

In the private health insurance market the government announced the following changes:

- the introduction of a compulsory health insurance for all insured people not in sickness funds;
- open enrolment requirements;
- premium regulation involving a minimum premium and a maximum premium.

Because the regulatory regime of the AWBZ, despite all the reform proposals since 1988, has not been much affected in the last seven years, in practice the adjustment of the reform proposal does not imply great changes with respect to the AWBZ. Major changes in practice can be expected in the coming years as a result of the proposed changes within the sickness fund and within the private health insurance sector.

What perspective?

As mentioned before, a crucial aspect of the government's proposal is to increase the financial responsibility of the sickness funds from 3 to 100 per cent of the difference between their actual expenses and the risk-adjusted predicted expenditures (except for the fixed hospitals costs). Undoubtedly this will bring new dynamics into the health care sector. It will yield premium competition among sickness funds and also more managed care activities. However, as long as the risk-adjusted capitation payments do not sufficiently reflect an individual's predictable future expenditures, sickness funds might be inclined to cream skim, with all its adverse effects.[11] Therefore, the government should be cautious in increasing the sickness funds' financial risk too much without simultaneously improving the risk-adjustment mechanism. What is important is that the government makes it credible that over time the risk-adjustment mechanism will be improved, and consequently the financial risk for the sickness funds will increase. This will stimulate sickness funds to make long term investments in managed care. If in the short term the financial risk of the sickness funds is tenfold of what it is today, without any cream skimming, the government will have made huge progress.

The government also announced plans to increase the financial risk for private health insurance companies, especially for the expenditures of persons aged 65 years and older. Currently all expenditures for these persons are fully reimbursed retrospectively. Consequently the insurance companies have no financial incentive for efficiency with respect to these costs. In order to guarantee financial access to private health insurance for everyone, the government also announced the introduction of open enrolment and premium regulation (minimum and maximum premiums) in the private health insurance market. However, in a competitive market with risk-bearing insurers, such regulation has to be supplemented by a risk-equalization scheme in order to compensate insurers for the predictable losses on high-risk insured people, especially when the proportion of high-risk insured people varies between insurers, as is currently the case in the Netherlands. In practice, the implementation of such a risk-equalization scheme is not only technically complicated, but is also a very sensitive issue politically.

Although the major adjustment of the Dekker–Simons proposals – that is two regulatory regimes instead of one – appeared to have a broad support in Parliament and in the health care sector, a fundamental discussion can be expected in the coming years of the advantages and disadvantages of having one or two regulatory regimes within the compulsory health insurance scheme. In the previous seven years the then governments put forward the following arguments against having two regulatory regimes instead of one:

- Where exactly should we draw the boundary between types of care for which the insurers bear and do not bear financial responsibility?
- How can we prevent insurers encouraging substitution of expensive care for which they do not bear any financial responsibility, for less expensive care for which they do bear financial responsibility (or that they block substitution the other way around)?
- How can we prevent closely interrelated forms of care being artificially separated by different financing mechanisms and different regulations?
- How can we deal with the complexity of two regulatory regimes?

It is remarkable that the new government announced the two regulatory regime, but did not give any clear arguments for it.

Nevertheless, the government made a correct decision for the following reasons. First, there is no prospect, at least within the next five years, of a workable system of risk-adjusted capitation payments for catastrophic risks. Second, even if there is a good risk-adjustment mechanism, a major problem might be that competing risk-bearing insurers have a financial incentive for skimping the quality of certain types of care. By quality skimping we mean the reduction of the quality of care to a level which is below the minimum level that is acceptable to society.

Although there are several good arguments why a regulated competitive market for health insurance may increase the quality of care (especially for the non-catastrophic risks), these arguments may not hold for two categories of care: first, care that is regularly used by persons who do not have the (mental) ability to make a trade-off between price and quality; and second, care about which many people are indifferent concerning quality because they ignore the low but positive probability of needing it during the next contract period.[12] Examples of these types of care are: institutional care for people with mental handicaps, long-term institutional care for physically handicapped people, chronic psychiatric care, long-term care for alcohol and drug addicts and long-term nursing home care.

Most of these types of care can be labelled as catastrophic risks. Although the government's decision to have two regulatory regimes is sensible, at least for the time being, a fundamental discussion is needed about the exact boundaries of the two regimes.

Finally, the government announced an ambitious time schedule for implementing its proposals. Undoubtedly, this is much too optimistic. However, more important than the realization of the time schedule, is to make steps in the right direction. The balanced way of thinking of the government about market and non-market elements in health care is promising.

LEARNING FROM THE DUTCH EXPERIENCE

In this chapter we have presented an overview of seven years of market-oriented reforms of the Dutch health care system. Although major changes have already taken place, the implementation process is far behind schedule because of resistance from interest groups and the technical and political complexity of the reforms. A first lesson from the Dutch reforms is that it is very hard to make a realistic time schedule for the full realization of such radical reforms. The implementation period originally projected was four years. A more realistic timetable would be at least 10 to 15 years. However, such a time schedule for a politically sensitive issue like health care and its financing is hard to realize for a cabinet that is in office for only four years. On the other hand, if in 1988 a realistic time schedule had been presented, it is doubtful whether all the changes that have been realized in the last years under the pressure of a tight time schedule, would have been achieved.

A second lesson is that the Dutch proposal for market-oriented health care is not a proposal for a free health care market. A free market in health care would yield effects that in most societies are considered undesirable. In a free health care market most low-income people and chronically ill people would not have financial access to all the care they need. It is important to realize that the Dutch government formulated a proposal for *regulated* competition. Government regulation will not fade away, but its emphasis will change dramatically. Instead of direct government control over volume, prices and productive capacity, the government will have to create the necessary conditions in order to prevent the undesired effects of a free market and to let the market achieve society's goal with respect to health care. Access to good quality care for the whole population is a major goal. The emphasis of government regulation will therefore be primarily on compulsory health insurance for everyone, on the risk-adjusted capitation payments to insurers, anti-cartel measures, quality control and disclosure of information. It is better to describe the Dutch health care reforms as 're-regulation' instead of 'de-regulation'.

A third lesson from the experience with the Dutch health care reforms is that a system of risk-adjusted capitation payments is a necessary condition in order to let such reforms be successful. In the Netherlands we are now in a vicious circle. In 1993 and 1994 sickness funds received an age–gender adjusted payment for each insured person. In 1995 region and disability were added as risk-adjusters. Because of the inaccuracy of the risk-adjusted capitation payments sickness funds are made responsible for only 3 per cent of the difference between their actual expenses and the risk-adjusted predicted expenses. However, as long as the government bears responsibility for the remaining 97 per cent, it does not want to give up the old tools for cost containment. Sickness funds, in turn, reproach the government for providing them with financial risks without giving them sufficient tools for cost-containment. This vicious circle can only be broken if the government provides the insurers with a serious prospect of a workable system of sufficiently risk-adjusted capitation payments.

Based on evidence from empirical research[13] we are optimistic about the technical feasibility of a sufficiently risk-adjusted capitation payment formula for the non-catastrophic risks (like hospital care, physician services and drugs). However, the practical implementation of such a payment system requires a considerable effort in data collection, research and administrative organization. Because of a lack of relevant research, we cannot draw any conclusion about the technical possibility of finding a risk-adjusted capitation payment formula for catastrophic risks, like long-term nursing home care and long-term institutional care for mentally and physically handicapped persons. At least in the first five years of the reforms, the Dutch government has severely underestimated the relevance of risk-adjusted capitation payments.

NOTES

1 A.C. Enthoven (1978) Consumer-choice health plan; A national-health-insurance proposal based on regulated competition in the

private sector. *New England Journal of Medicine*, 298: 709–20; W. Dekker (1987) *Willingness to Change*. The Hague: SDU.

2 Ministry of Welfare, Health, and Cultural Affairs (1988) *Verandering verzekerd*. Tweede Kamer, 1987–88, 19945 (27–8).

3 F.T. Schut (1992) Workable competition in health care: Prospects for the Dutch design. *Social Science and Medicine*, 35, 1445–55.

4 Ministry of Welfare, Health, and Cultural Affairs (1990) *Werken aan zorgvernieuwing*. Tweede Kamer, 1989–1990, 21545 (2), May. The Hague: SDU.

5 E. Elsinga (1989) Political decision-making in health care: The Dutch case. *Health Policy*, 11, 243–55.

6 A. Wagstaf and E.K.A. van Doorslaer (1992) Equity in the finance of health care: Some international comparisons. *Journal of Health Economics*, 11, 361–87.

7 F.T. Schut (1992) Workable competition in heath care: Prospects for the Dutch design. *Social Science and Medicine*, 35: 1445–55.

8 W.P.M.M. van de Ven and R.C.J.A. van Vliet (1992) How can we prevent cream skimming in a competitive health insurance market? The great challenge for the 90s, in P. Zweifel and H.E. Frech (eds) *Health Economics Worldwide*. Dordrecht: Kluwer: 23–46.

9 Ministry of Health, Wealth and Sport (1995) *Kostenbeheersing in de zorgsector*. Tweede Kamer, 1994–95, 24124 (1–2), March. The Hague: SDU.

10 Biesheuvel Committee (1994) *Gedeelde zorg: betere zorg*. Hageman, Zoetermeer.

11 W.P.M.M. van de Ven and R.C.J.A. van Vliet (1992) How can we prevent cream skimming in a competitive health insurance market? The great challenge for the 90s, in P. Zweifel and H.E. Frech (eds) *Health Economics Worldwide*. Dordrecht: Kluwer: 23–46.

12 W.P.M.M. van de Ven and R.C.J.A. van Vliet (1992) How can we prevent cream skimming in a competitive health insurance market? The great challenge for the 90s, in P. Zweifel and H.E. Frech (eds) *Health Economics Worldwide*. Dordrecht: Kluwer: 23–46; W.P.M.M. van de Ven and F.T. Schut (1994) Should catastrophic risks be included in a regulated competitive health insurance market? *Social Science and Medicine*, 29, 1459–72.

13 W.P.M.M. van de Ven, R.C.J.A. van Vliet, E.M. van Barneveld and L.L. Lamers (1994) Risk-adjusted capitation: Recent experiences in the Netherlands, *Health Affairs* 13 (5): 120–36.

6

GERMANY
Friedrich Wilhelm Schwartz and Reinhard Busse

INTRODUCTION

You cannot understand the German health care system if you do not know about federalism and corporatism. Both are fundamental principles of German politics – inside as well as outside the health care system (see Figure 6.1). Federalism is the basic structural principle of Germany which by constitution is formed by its 16 member states, the so-called Länder. Corporatism has several important aspects: first, it hands over certain legally defined rights of the state to self-governing institutions. Second, these institutions have mandatory membership and the right to raise their own financial resources under the auspices of, and more or less regulated by, the state. Third, the corporatist institutions have the right and obligation to negotiate and sign contracts with other institutions and to finance or deliver services to their members.

The contrasting principle to both federalism and corporatism is etatism which in principle means the central state regulates directly. In Germany, the constitution mandates that living conditions shall be of equal standard in all Länder. The central state therefore tries to set uniform rules. The federal Länder and the corporatist institutions, on the other hand, seek to develop their own rules.

In the health care system, we can identify the major actors representing these three principles (see Figure 6.2). At the central level, the Federal Ministry of Health is the key player, as from time to time is the Parliament. Federalism is represented mainly by the 16 state governments and (but in fact to a very small extent) by the state parliaments. Corporatism is represented through the sickness

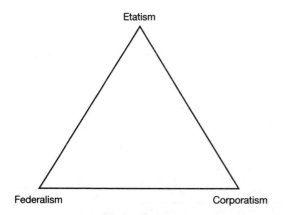

Figure 6.1 Fundamental principles of German politics

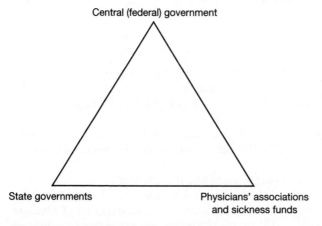

Figure 6.2 Major actors in the health care system

funds' associations on the purchaser side and the physicians' and dentists' associations on the provider side. Both have mandatory membership. The purchaser side is made up of about 600 autonomous sickness funds which are organized on a regional and federal basis. Physicians' associations exist in every state following the principles of federalism. To make matters more complicated, hospitals are not represented by any legal institution.

All of these actors have defined missions (see Figure 6.3). Equity, comprehensiveness and setting the rules and frame for financing

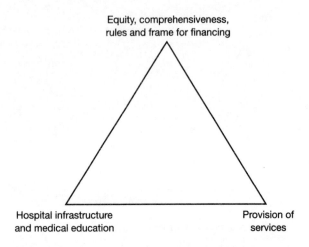

Equity, comprehensiveness,
rules and frame for financing

Hospital infrastructure
and medical education

Provision of
services

Figure 6.3   Missions of actors in the health care system

health care are the responsibility of the central state. The German social code book regulates the following items:

- mandatory and voluntary membership in sickness funds;
- the scope of the sickness funds' benefit package;
- the organizational structure of sickness funds and their associations;
- the goals and scope of negotiations between the sickness funds and providers of health care, most notably the physicians' associations; and
- financing mechanisms, including the division of contributions to the sickness funds between employers and employees, definition of fixed budgets for certain sectors, and distribution of revenue and expenses between the sickness funds according to a defined compensatory mechanism.

Membership of a sickness fund is compulsory for workers whose gross income does not exceed a certain level and voluntary for those above that level and the self-employed. Although the general principles have been in place since the introduction of social insurance in 1883, mandatory membership has been extended to dependants, retired persons, farmers, the unemployed, students and others over the decades. Currently, of the 88 per cent of the population covered, 75 per cent are mandatory members and their dependants, while 13 per cent are voluntary members and their dependants. All mandatory members of a particular sickness fund contribute the same percentage of their income which at the beginning of 1996 was on average 13.4 per cent although percentages vary between 9 per cent and 15 per cent, shared between employees and employers.

Benefits for the insured population were improved constantly until the early 1970s. The last major steps included full wages during periods of sickness, the abolition of sickness days without wages in 1969, and the inclusion of preventative services in 1970. The Benefits Improvement Act 1973 which ended limited hospital care coverage was even passed after the beginning of the first oil crisis, although in practice the oil crisis marked the end of the golden era of Germany's social welfare expansion. Currently, sickness funds coverage includes prevention of disease, screening for disease and treatment of disease. Treatment includes ambulatory medical care, dental care, drugs, non-physicians' care, medical devices, in-patient care, nursing care at home, and rehabilitation. In addition to these benefits in kind, sickness funds give cash benefits for the first six weeks in which employers are responsible for the sick pay. A further benefit is health promotion which is offered by sickness funds directly outside the uniform benefits' package.

The Länder governments are responsible for hospital building. They do so by preparing hospital plans and paying for investments of hospitals listed in those plans. They are also responsible for undergraduate medical education and the supervision of both the physicians' offices and associations. The corporatist institutions have the obligation to secure the actual provision of all health care services. The most prominent examples of this are the physicians' and dentists' associations which both have a corporate monopoly and mission to secure ambulatory care. The main elements of the corporatist monopoly and mission are the obligation to meet the health needs of the population, to provide state-wide services in all medical specialties, and to receive a fixed budget from the sickness funds which the physicians' associations distribute among their members.

This is the corporatist 'secret' explaining Germany's successful cost-containment strategies in the ambulatory care sector which includes – unlike that in the UK or the Netherlands – every specialty. Because of the absence of corporatist institutions in the hospital sector, hospitals contract individually with the sickness funds' organizations. This also explains why cost-containment policies are still not working in the hospital sector. In addition, the absence of corporatist institutions in the hospital sector on one side, and the

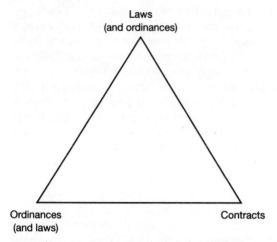

Figure 6.4   Tools used by actors in the health care system

monopoly for ambulatory care on the other, is a major part of the reason for the almost complete separation between in-patient and out-patient care in Germany.

The tools used by each actor for its specific mission vary (see Figure 6.4). The main tool of central government is laws, primarily the social code book V and the reform laws changing it. Included in this legislation is the power of the Minister of Health to issue ordinances, for example to set the growth rates of the fixed budgets. For the state governments, ordinances are much more important. One example was the nomination of a state commissioner to run Lower Saxony's dentists' association in July 1995 which – in a conflict for money and more importantly power – did not comply with the contracts negotiated with the sickness funds following the principles of the social code book.

This complicated system of triangulated power may not be easy to understand but it has been working for over 100 years. In the following sections we will outline the development and the main functions of corporatism in the ambulatory care sector in more detail.

HISTORICAL DEVELOPMENT

When the German Reichsversicherungsordnung (RVO) had been passed and the statutory health insurance scheme was founded in

1883, the sickness funds were responsible for the provision of health services for their relatively few insured members. The sickness funds either employed doctors themselves or determined the prices for their services. When the statutory health insurance became compulsory for more occupational groups and later for dependants and retired persons, the number of insured people grew to such an extent that the physicians formed organizations in order to improve their bargaining positions. They also began to question the monopoly of the sickness funds. Initially, the government did not react. It left the settlement of the conflict to the sickness funds, and this caused the formation of associations on their side.

When the physicians threatened to go on a country-wide strike in 1913, the government, in spite of the threat to the system, again did not respond by issuing a decree on how the provision of health care should be guaranteed, but advanced a defensive settlement of the conflict in the shape of a civil law contract between the sickness funds' associations on the one side and the organization of doctors on the other. This so-called 'Berliner Abkommen' not only determined a minimum number of doctors per insured persons but also established committees with equal representation of sickness funds and physicians for the accreditation of sickness fund affiliated doctors. In this way, the fundamental principles were elaborated in a law-free area by self-governing bodies in long and fierce discussions. They were later modified and refined by the legislature, but are still in force today.

During the Weimar Republic, the strategy of intervening as little as possible into the management of health care provision was maintained. The procedure of collective negotiations which seemed to represent the minimum of government intervention was successful. The ministerial bureaucracy usually solved problems which arose through negotiations or by creating institutions with both sides represented. After the expiry of the 'Berliner Abkommen' in 1923, the National Committee of Physicians and Sickness Funds was created by an emergency decree. The establishment of this body, in which the leading groups had to work together, was the equivalent of an approval of collective negotiations as an instrument for central regulation.

Walter Spielhagen, a major official of the Reich Ministry for Work, explained this in the following way:

> Founded on the experience that the Reichstag is not the right place to solve the numerous questions on the purpose of the

relation between doctors and health insurance funds, the legislature transmitted a part of its own responsibilities in this small
but important field to a body with equal representation. By
giving this body certain responsibilities under public law, the
legislature turns the involved associations from objects to sub-
jects of legislation.[1]

Physicians' associations with a claim on common payments and
with the monopoly and mission to provide and guarantee ambulatory health care were created by an emergency decree in 1931.
This was not only the end of the sickness funds' *de facto* mission to
provide health care but also the end of direct relations between
sickness funds and individual physicians. The physicians' associations became the crucial interface between sickness funds on one
side and medical care on the other.

The approval of the physicians' associations as public corporations by a decree of the National Socialist regime in 1933 created a
structure that integrated the collective negotiations of sickness
funds' associations and physicians' corporations within the statutory health insurance scheme. In the Third Reich itself, however,
this structure did not come to fruition because both sides, like all
other institutions, were brought into line by the Nazi party and had
to act accordingly. In 1955, after the foundation of the Federal
Republic of Germany, the structure was taken up again and was
developed further.

In summary, the corporatist mission and monopoly developed
out of the idea of governmental self-restriction in view of the
variety of details connected with the question of physicians in the
statutory health insurance scheme. This is all the more important as
it does not represent a lack of interest of the Weimar State in its
citizens' health. The Weimar Constitution clearly underlined that
health is a state responsibility which is to be put into effect by a
social insurance scheme.

CENTRAL ASPECTS OF THE CORPORATIST MISSION

The central aspects of the corporatist mission to secure ambulatory
care will be explained by means of its central concepts, namely
meeting the health needs, the guarantee to provide services and
total payment.

Meeting the health needs

Legally, the physicians' associations have to guarantee an evenly distributed and needs-adapted provision of health care, including the provision of sufficient emergency services within reasonable distances.[2] This definition, introduced in 1976, replaced the old target of an adequate provision of health care and put it into concrete form. This concept of meeting the health needs means in fact the prohibition of insufficient health care for sickness funds' members.

Related to the concept of meeting the health needs is the demand for an even distribution of health services that adapts and interprets the principle of equal chances for health in the German constitution. Even distribution includes a geographical equality in the supply of health services and provision policy. It also includes the concept of social equality, that is equality in spite of differences in income and social class. This supplements the proportional, income-related contributions based on the principle of solidarity and the method of providing services with third party reimbursement which was introduced in order to prevent problems in choosing and seeing a doctor. All this demonstrates the value which is assigned to social equality in the German health care system and it is complemented by the protection of equality in medical care by means of equal fees for physicians' services.

Guarantee to provide services

The physicians' associations have to provide health services as defined by the legislature and they have to guarantee the sickness funds that this provision meets the legal and contracted requirements. This releases the sickness funds from permanent and direct checking as to whether the mission of health care provision is fulfilled by the affiliated physicians. The physicians' associations, on the other hand, are legally obliged to supervise every single one of their members through numerous and extensive duties in participation, documentation and checking, which are laid down in detail. Because of these specific rights to intervene and control, the physicians' associations were constructed as self-governing bodies. This facilitates their work which is constantly influenced by the doctors' freedom of diagnosis and therapy and supports the principle of a democratically legitimized cooperative. If the sickness funds could not avail themselves of these services and this guarantee given by the physicians' associations, they would have to use their own medical services.

Total payment

The sickness funds render total payments for the remuneration of the affiliated doctors to the physicians' associations. This releases them from the duty to pay the doctors directly. The physicians' associations have to distribute these total payments according to the unified value scale and their regulations on the distribution of payments. The physicians' associations have to check, record and sum up the data that form the basis of these calculations. Before the appearance of sensational cases of fraud by a few doctors in the 1980s, some physicians' associations did not even transmit the record cards to the sickness funds – they just gave them total numbers.

The method of total payment is not only an administrative relief for the sickness funds. In view of the increase in total expenditure of the statutory health insurance system, it enabled the Federal Physicians' Association and the sickness funds' associations to develop recommendations for limits on the total payment for doctors. The first decisive effects were achieved almost immediately.[3] From a structural policy's point of view it is remarkable that these associations developed the method of agreements on global recommendations and successfully pushed it through bilaterally.

CURRENT REFORMS

In Germany, there has been a continuing discussion on cost control in the health care system. This has resulted in an almost permanent process of law making. Sometimes those laws were termed cost containment laws (as in 1977), sometimes they had the same intention but were not named as such. It is neither possible nor useful to discuss details of this step-wise learning and interaction process. Instead, we will briefly recap the most important cost containment measures introduced by the latest laws, namely the Health Care Reform Act of 1989 and the Health Care Structure Act of 1993. The most significant reason for reform was the period of deep and relatively long recession combined with the additional economic burden of the German unification. In addition, we will try to examine the consequences of these two reform laws for the balance of power in the German health care system.

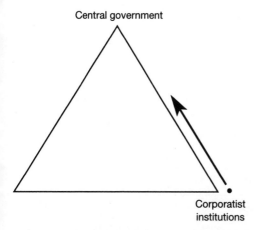

Central government

Corporatist
institutions

Figure 6.5   The power shift in ambulatory care

As already mentioned, the ambulatory care sector is the traditional stronghold of the corporatist institutions. This was also the only sector in which cost containment measures were introduced more or less voluntarily through negotiated budgets since 1976. Following the Health Care Reform Act of 1989, the sickness funds and the physicians' associations were obliged to reach such agreements on fixed budgets for each region under the condition that the contribution rate of the sickness funds' members would remain constant. The Health Care Structure Act of 1993 further restricted the growth rate of these budgets by law to the level of growth in the contributory income until 1995.[4] In short, we observe a shift in power from the corporatist institutions towards central government (see Figure 6.5). In spite of the physicians' demand for the abolition of fixed budgets in the next health care reform law, it appears to be most likely that we will return to negotiated but fixed budgets in the future.

The in-patient sector was relatively unaffected by the Health Care Reform Act of 1989. This was due largely to the fact that the German Länder viewed hospital policy as their domain and were unwilling to lose control of it. The Health Care Structure Act of 1993 caused major changes in the financing of hospitals. These changes took place in two phases. In the first phase, from 1993 until 1995, budgets were fixed at the individual hospital level. The growth in these budgets was formally controlled by the Federal Ministry of

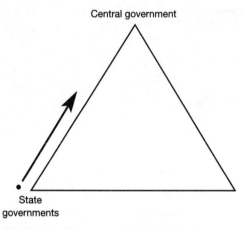

Figure 6.6   The power shift in hospital care

Health. However, because there were a lot of exceptions, hospital costs rose twice as fast as the contributory incomes.

Since 1996, this financing system has been replaced by a mixed system made up of three components: case fees, procedure fees and department-specific per diem rates. Case fees covering the entire hospital period have been introduced for the first time, mainly for surgical cases. Procedure fees, which are paid on top of the per diem rates, already existed but there are now 140 instead of 16. Procedure fees are paid both for major surgery such as transplants and for minor procedures like the insertion of a pacemaker. It is noteworthy that case and procedure fees are set by the Federal Ministry of Health which will leave only department-specific per diem rates for negotiation. These have replaced the hospital-wide per diem rates.[5]

In summary, power has shifted towards central government and away from the state governments (see Figure 6.6). Currently, two questions are of particular relevance: what will be the consequences of the prospective payment system in terms of equity, quality, and costs? Will the Federal Minister of Health succeed with his proposal to constitute corporatist institutions in the hospital sector from 1997 which would then be responsible for keeping to regional hospital care budgets negotiated with the sickness funds? In the meantime, fixed hospital budgets have been extended from 1996 with far fewer exceptions.

The pharmaceutical sector was relatively unregulated before the most recent reform laws. Pharmaceutical companies offered a large

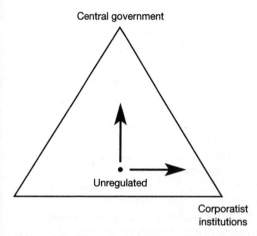

Figure 6.7 The power shift in the pharmaceutical sector

range of drugs at prices only they determined. The first major legal regulation was the introduction of reference prices for commonly used drugs which marked the upper limit for the costs reimbursable through the sickness funds. In 1993, fixed budgets were laid down for the pharmaceutical sector as well as for the medical devices and products sector. The amounts of these budgets were originally set by the Health Care Structure Act of 1993, that is by the federal parliament. For 1993, budgets were fixed at the 1991 level, approximately 10 per cent lower than actual spending in 1992. Yearly growth rates can be negotiated between the sickness funds and the physicians' associations but the first increases were set for 1995. In the case of overspending, the regional physicians' associations are liable for the debt.[6] Since expenditure was kept within the budget in 1993 and largely in 1994 and 1995, government officials view this policy as a success. On the other hand, considerable overspendings are predicted for the future and subsequently a reduction in physicians' earnings. All of these regulations constitute an obvious shift of influence towards both the central level and the corporatist institutions (see Figure 6.7). Research has so far not produced a conclusive picture about the outcomes of the drug budget on other budgets.

The main changes induced by the ongoing reform process affecting the sickness funds are the financial pooling of their risks in two stages. The first was the sharing of the expenditure for the retired amongst all sickness funds. In the second, introduced by the Health Care Structure Act of 1993, contributions are allocated to the sickness funds according to the sociodemographic characteristics of their members. The third step – starting in 1996 – is the introduction of an almost free choice of sickness fund for the members of the statutory health insurance scheme.

The cost containment laws of the 1980s, especially the Health Care Reform Act of 1989, restricted the sickness funds individually with regard to their negotiating power. This applied to their negotiations with the organizations of health care services providers, but also to the range of services that can be offered to the clients. The law almost entirely abolished the free scope of regulations that the sickness funds could define in their statutes before.

In their role as purchaser organizations, all sickness funds are obliged to pay the same prices in a uniform way for ambulatory and hospital care and for almost every other prescribed service. Competition, therefore, can only mean either numerous clients with high incomes – although profits partly have to be redistributed – or enhanced but cheaper administrative services, assuming that clients' price sensitivity plays any role in the sickness funds' competition for market share at all. In the course of the centralization of the sickness funds' external activities, the funds' rights to decide in joint committees with the providers as much as in negotiations with providers were strengthened step by step, but the principle of standardization of services for the insured population remained unchanged. This uniformity is even maintained where the last cost containment law created the possibility for sickness funds to take over the guarantee for the population's provision of health services. This is only possible, however, on condition that a majority of the contracted doctors cancels the compulsory membership in the cartel of the physicians' associations.

As a result, it is not surprising that the sickness funds are now pleading for more freedom to act and for more competition in terms of contracts. They are also asking for purchasing designs involving strong competition among the suppliers of health services, who are no longer forced to be members and thus are no longer bound to the compulsory alliance of service suppliers, as they are in the physicians' associations today.[7] The sickness funds are not mistaken if they talk about the 'dangerous logic of this system which is on its way to a one and single health insurance for all', meaning the centralization and standardization of all their activities.[8] They are also correct if they claim the right to make contracts with no obligations on uniformity in order to be able to respond to the increased demands of their clients to choose their insurance funds and offer them alternatives. These would then no longer be guided and bound both by legal professional associations and by unified and centralized comprehensive (almost population-wide) contract mechanisms. In fact, open clauses for alternative purchaser and insurance models of the managed care type – like HMOs – could mark the end of the traditional system of the uniformly balanced and regulated ambulatory and hospital services in Germany.

The Federal Minister of Health, Horst Seehofer, has apparently realized this conflict and wants to keep, in principle, uniform regulations on contracting mechanisms. On the other hand, in the discussion about a new health care reform law, it became evident that the trend towards centralization faced severe criticism. As a consequence, Seehofer promised in 1995 to give more power back to the self-governing corporations. However, forced by the Maastricht doctrine to reduce deficit spending, he still rated the principles of revenue oriented expenditure policy and stability of the contribution rate higher, and proposals to put a legal cap on both the employers' and the employees' share of the contribution were seriously discussed.

In May 1996, Seehofer pushed a legal reduction of contribution rates by 0.4 per cent from January 1997 to achieve the overall goal of the government – that is, to reduce additional costs on wages for the employers. The forced reduction in sickness funds' expenditure – which is supposed to amount to 3 per cent of total expenditure – will be made possible by reducing benefits (for example, by offering three weeks' rehabilitation instead of four weeks', and 70 per cent sick pay instead of 80 per cent) and increasing co-payments for rehabilitation, pharmaceuticals, dentures, spectacles and other services. In addition, Seehofer proposed to eliminate health promotion as a sickness fund benefit. Surprisingly enough he launched an attempt to enforce competition between sickness funds by giving them more freedom to decide about the benefits later in 1996.

CONCLUSION

It remains to be seen whether the traditional German mechanisms and principles – which could be considered as a possible or intended successful outcome of a reform process in a lot of other countries – will survive or even be strengthened in this current conflict between regulation and competition.

NOTES

1 T. Lauer-Kirschbaum (1994) Kollektivverhandlungen und Selbstverwaltungskonsens: Interessenegoismus und Gemeinwohlorientierung in der Entwicklung und Reform der gesetzlichen Krankenversicherung, in B. Blanke (ed.) *Krankheit und Gemeinwohl.* Obladen: Leske und Budrich: 207–44.

2 H. Bogs (1982) Selbstverwaltung im gesundheitsökonomischen Planungssystem der gesetzlichen Krankenversicherung, in H. Bogs, P. Herder-Dorneich, E.K. Scheuch and G.W. Wittkämper *Gesundheitspolitik zwischen Staat und Selbstverwaltung.* Köln: Deutscher Ärzteverlag: 415–80.

3 P. Herder-Dorneich (1982) Sozialökonomische Entwicklungen im Gesundheitswesen, ihre Auswirkungen auf den ambulanten Sektor und ihre ordnungspolitische Steuerung, in H. Bogs, P. Herder-Dorneich, E.K. Scheuch and G.W. Wittkämper *Gesundheitspolitik zwischen Staat und Selbstverwaltung.* Köln: Deutscher Ärzteverlag: 133–236.

4 F.W. Schwartz and R. Busse (1996) Fixed budgets in the ambulatory care sector: the German experience, in F.W. Schwartz, H. Glennerster and R.B. Saltman (eds) *Fixing Health Budgets – Experiences from Europe and North America.* Chichester: Wiley & Sons: 93–108.

5 M. Pfaff and D. Wassener (1995) *Das Krankenhaus im Gefolge des Gesundheits – Struktur – Gesetzes 1993.* Baden-Baden: Nomos.

6 R. Busse and C. Howorth (1996). Fixed budgets in the pharmaceutical sector in Germany: Effects on cost and quality, in F.W. Schwartz, H. Glennerster and R.B. Saltman (eds) *Fixing Health Budgets – Experience from Europe and North America.* Chichester: Wiley & Sons: 109–27.

7 S. Richard and K-H. Schönbach (1996) German sickness funds under fixed budgets, in F.W. Schwartz, H. Glennerster and R.B. Saltman (eds) *Fixing Health Budgets – Experience from Europe and North America.* Chichester: Wiley & Sons: 187–201.

8 H. Rebscher (1994) Solidarische Wettbewerbsordnung. *Arbeit und Sozialpolitik,* No. 1/2: 42–8.

7

LESSONS AND CONCLUSIONS

Chris Ham

The chapters presented in this book illustrate the developing pattern of health care reform in Europe and the United States. While the detail of reform is specific to individual countries, a number of common themes emerge. Not surprisingly, many of these themes take us back to the discussion in Chapter 1 on the background to health care reform and the policies adopted in this process. In this conclusion, we bring together the material presented in earlier chapters in a thematic overview of experience so far and the lessons that can be distilled from this experience. We also go beyond the discussions in the country chapters to draw on other studies to offer a broader commentary on the evolution of reforms and possible future directions. The chapter begins with some reflections on the way in which reforms were implemented.

LESSONS ABOUT THE PROCESS OF REFORM

One of the values of comparative studies is in highlighting variations between systems. In relation to the experiences reported in this book, it is clear that one of the most important sources of variation is in the *process* of reform itself. Four approaches can be identified.

First, there is what has been described as 'big bang reform'.[1] This is illustrated by the United Kingdom where the reforms devised by the Thatcher government were introduced in a short period of time and were driven through by a government committed to their implementation. Between 1989 when the reforms were announced and 1996 the organization of the NHS was transformed as the old centrally planned system gave way to a pluralistic organization based more on networks than hierarchies. Other countries that have experienced big bang reform are Israel and New Zealand.

Second, there is 'incremental reform'. This is exemplified by the approach adopted in the Netherlands which was much more cautious than that pursued in the United Kingdom. The Dutch government translated Plan-Dekker into Plan-Simons and this has since been superseded by the changes announced in 1995. Even at the end of almost 10 years of reform, many of the key proposals in the Dekker report have not been implemented, and now may never be taken forward. The Dutch political system, based on coalition governments and a greater emphasis on consensus than is apparent in the United Kingdom, helps to explain this difference of approach. Germany has also embarked on the path of incremental reform.

Third, there is 'bottom up reform'. This description best fits Sweden where the decentralized nature of the system has led to important variations between county councils in the policies that have been pursued. To a greater extent than in other systems, reforms in Sweden have been driven from the bottom up rather than the top down. There have, of course, been a number of national policy initiatives, but the pace has been set by innovative politicians in the county councils and the role of national government has been somewhat less important than in other European systems. As a result, Sweden has experienced a number of natural experiments.

Fourth, there is 'reform without reform'. The United States illustrates this approach where rapid changes continue to occur despite the defeat of the Clintons' plans. As in Sweden, this is partly a consequence of the decentralized nature of health services in the United States, but more importantly it reflects the highly pluralistic system of health care in that country and the organic process of reform that characterizes such a system. A further similarity with Sweden is that the nature and pace of reform varies within the United States with some states experiencing rapid and profound changes while others evolve much more slowly.

A further lesson follows, namely that the implementation stage of reform is at least as important as the formulation stage in explaining what happens in practice. In the United Kingdom, the Thatcher government's proposals were sketched in broad outline only and the detail was added in the course of implementation. This has been described as an emergent strategy or the government making it up as they were going along.[2] The implementation process was also important in the other countries whose experiences have been described here with key aspects of the original proposals being adapted, amended or reversed in the implementation stage. This reflects gaps in the original policy designs as well as a commitment to learning by doing. It also demonstrates how those responsible for implementation at a decentralized level were able to shape the content and direction of reforms. Implementation was influenced too by important changes in the personnel responsible for steering the reforms. In some cases, this meant that the more radical aspirations of earlier reformers were modified in practice both through a process of political bargaining and through the influence of those responsible for implementation. The nature of the bargaining process was in some cases driven by ideology and in others by bureaucratic and professional politics. In extreme cases, as in the United States, this meant that reforms were stillborn. Whatever the particular conjuncture of circumstances, the effect was to modify, often quite significantly, the path of change.

To make this point is to demonstrate that policies create politics.[3] In other words, policies developed in one period give rise to a set of relationships between organizations and interests in the health care system, and this in turn shapes the development of future policies. Kirkman-Liff's metaphor of the hardening cement expresses the same point more graphically: in the United States, reform becomes more difficult over time and movement eventually ceases as it proves impossible for reformers to take further steps through the cement. The United States is not alone in this respect. The experience of Germany reported here also shows the importance of the established pattern of political relationships on policy development, although unlike the United States it suggests that opposition to change can be overcome if the political will exists. In the United States, the separation of powers and the ability to veto legislation at so many different points means that policies are formulated in an alligator-infested swamp (to vary the metaphor) and their chances of survival in this environment are limited in the extreme. By contrast, in the United Kingdom a government with a parliamentary majority was able to push ahead rapidly with its policies in the face of opposition because the existence of a unitary political system limited the opportunities for opponents to frustrate these policies.

The rapidly evolving vocabulary of reforms is one of the most noteworthy aspects of recent changes. The language used by policy makers has fluctuated depending on the political parties in government and the perception by politicians of reaction to their plans. Most obviously, words such as competition, purchasers and contracts have given way to collaboration, commissioners and service agreements. This applies not only in the United Kingdom but also in the Netherlands. As van de Ven shows in his chapter, by altering the vocabulary of reform in this way it was possible to maintain support for the changes made to the Dutch system despite shifts in the governing coalition. In the United Kingdom, the use of different words to describe the reforms was convenient not only to the Labour Party as it developed its health policy but also to Conservative health ministers who did not always have the courage of their predecessors' convictions and who were in any case concerned to respond to evidence of public disenchantment with market oriented solutions to put a different spin on their policies.

One of the paradoxes about the reforms is that changes which were ostensibly designed to result in greater decentralization and a bigger role for markets sometimes had the opposite effect. Schwartz and Busse show how in Germany the tradition of self-regulation by the associations representing doctors, dentists and sickness funds, and the powerful position of regional governments, has been eroded as a result of increasing intervention by the federal government. Similarly, in Sweden, the decision of the government to allow doctors the freedom to set up in practice acted as a constraint on the county councils. A more mixed pattern is apparent in the United Kingdom where the autonomy given to NHS trusts and general practitioner fundholders was matched by increasing central control over key policy objectives, such as the reduction in waiting lists. In this case, centralization on some issues went hand in hand with decentralization on others in a style of political management that defied description in the terms usually deployed for this purpose.

As our analysis has shown, technical complexities also arose during the implementation process. Most obviously, in the Dutch case, van de Ven illustrates the challenges involved in developing a risk adjusted capitation formula for allocating resources to insurers. This contributed to the slow pace of implementation in the Netherlands and also led to the decision to maintain a separation between insurance for catastrophic illnesses and for other illnesses. Technical factors were important too in the United States where it has been argued that the complexity of the Clintons' proposals contributed to their downfall. The detailed design work that went into the Clintons' proposals stands in stark contrast to the United Kingdom where, as we have noted, the Thatcher government's proposals were lacking in detail and where policy making took place 'on the hoof'. This comparison gives the lie to the argument that implementation follows smoothly if the technical obstacles to reform are anticipated and addressed. As this book has shown, the politics of health care reform are arguably more important than the science and it would be wrong to assume that a simple set of prescriptions can be developed to guide reformers through the maze. In reality, health care reform raises a whole series of value judgements which can only be resolved as part of a process of debate and discussion. As we noted in Chapter 1, at the heart of this process is the need to make trade-offs between different values and objectives.

EMERGING LESSONS

What then does the experience of reform tell us about the effectiveness of different strategies?[4] We begin with a negative lesson. As Kirkman-Liff shows in his contribution, if basic social goals such as access to health care for all groups in the population and equity in service provision are considered important, then the United States approach to health care financing and delivery should not be emulated. Notwithstanding the provision of high standards of care to many people and outstanding examples of clinical innovation and excellence, the United States is the only country in this study that has yet to guarantee universal or near universal population coverage. The failure of the Clintons' reforms, whatever their merits, means that this goal is unlikely to be achieved in the foreseeable future. As a consequence, millions of Americans are either uninsured or underinsured and have to rely on the limited safety net provisions available in that country. While there are lessons to be drawn from the United States experience at the micro level, and we reflect on these further below, as a system its negative characteristics outweigh the positives.

Kirkman-Liff's assessment is therefore a timely reminder to Europeans: whatever the shortcomings of your systems, recognize the progress already made in ensuring access to necessary medical care for the population and working towards equity. This conclusion is underscored by evidence that the United States is also the most costly health care system in the world with a significant proportion of health care expenditure (currently comprising over 14 per cent of GDP) accounted for by the administrative overheads associated with voluntary health insurance and competitive health care markets. Other systems that have used this funding method have encountered similar problems. As Hsiao notes in his analysis:

> Any nation that contemplates relying on private insurance to finance basic health care would be well advised to study the history and experiences of the USA, Chile and the Philippines. Their unforeseen long-term negative consequences were much greater that any short-term relief that private insurance may have provided.[5]

From the European perspective, this suggests that the emphasis on funding health care mainly through public sources is the correct approach and that reform efforts should be targeted more at the delivery of care than its funding. In practice, of course, this is precisely what has happened. For seasoned health policy analysts, it may seem unnecessary to labour this point, but at a time when emerging democracies around the world look to the United States as a model to be copied, and when mature democracies are reconsidering the balance between state and personal responsibility, the weakness of private insurance as the *main* way of paying for health care bears repetition. This has been emphasized by other researchers for similar reasons.[6]

There is another lesson on health service finance, namely that cost containment strategies have been more successful in some countries than others. Leaving the United States on one side, we have seen that Sweden has been particularly effective in containing costs with the share of GDP allocated to health care actually falling in the 1980s. Part of the reason for this was the transfer of responsibility of care of the elderly from county councils to municipal councils, but nevertheless spending was reined in significantly. In contrast, Germany has continued to experience difficulties in keeping expenditure within budget, particularly in the hospital sector. This helps to explain the succession of reform laws that have been passed in Germany. The Netherlands and the United Kingdom have achieved greater success than Germany in this respect, although the increase in health service expenditure in the United Kingdom immediately following the introduction of the NHS reforms seemed to suggest, in support of Hurst, that expenditure is more difficult to control in contract based systems than in integrated systems. Subsequently, and echoing Abel-Smith's analysis, spending in the United Kingdom has been restrained through direct government intervention.[7]

The experience of the Netherlands, Sweden, the United Kingdom and Germany confirms the observation made in the introduction that in reforming the delivery of health care there has been a shift from the integrated to the contract model, interest in the use of market-like mechanisms and the deployment of a range of budgetary incentives to improve performance. Yet it is also apparent that there are differences between countries in how these ideas are being taken forward. For example, only Sweden and the United Kingdom have moved from an integrated approach to one based on contracts. Such a shift was not necessary in the Netherlands or Germany because in these social insurance systems the roles of insurers and providers has always been distinct. What has changed in the Netherlands and Germany is the requirement that sickness funds as insurers should take a more active role in their negotiations with providers and should contract selectively with them. In other words, echoing the argument of *Health Check*, the intention is that insurers should transform themselves from being relatively passive payers to become more discriminating and prudent purchasers.[8]

A key lesson from this book is the importance of the purchaser role in the contract model. This was not fully appreciated at the outset of recent reform efforts with the consequence that provider dominance of health care has persisted. Only latterly have policy makers woken up to the need to radically transform the role of purchasers – whether these were previously called insurers, health authorities, county councils or sickness funds. It has become increasingly apparent that there needs to be a countervailing force to the power of providers and that this will take time to develop. The significance of this insight is appreciated in the United States as well as Europe as organizations are established by public and private payers to negotiate with health plans.[9] In some parts of the United States, these purchasing groups appear to be having a significant effect on insurance premiums. The United Kingdom reforms are of particular interest in illustrating the emergence of both patient focused and population centred models of purchasing. The evidence indicates that each model has advantages and disadvantages and that the purchasing function is likely to be most effective if it combines elements of both.[10] A further development noted by van de Ven is the establishment of direct patient purchasing or personal budgeting in the Netherlands, the progress of which is certain to be followed closely elsewhere.

The Dutch initiative underlines the importance attached to patient choice by health care reformers. The extreme example of this is the United States where the concern of some interests to maintain choice was one of the factors that led to the defeat of the Clintons' plan. Choice is also a key objective in the European countries whose experiences have been reviewed here. This has always been the case in the Netherlands and Germany and it has been of increasing significance too in Sweden. In the case of Sweden, this is in part a reaction to a tradition in which patients have been expected to use the health centre or hospital nearest to where they live. Patients in Sweden now have almost complete freedom of doctor and hospital and the guarantee to reduce waiting times for treatment to a maximum of three months underlines the importance attached to improving access to services. Waiting time targets have also been set in the United Kingdom, although they are distinctly less ambitious. Furthermore, while the NHS reforms were launched by a white paper entitled *Working for Patients*, in practice patient choice has if anything been reduced rather than increased by the reforms. Kirkman-Liff notes how paradoxically this is also happening in the United States as a consequence of reform without reform, albeit from a very different starting point.

Patient choice of insurer has been encouraged in the Netherlands and Germany but not in Sweden. Public purchasers in Sweden have a monopoly in their areas, as do health authorities in the United Kingdom. The main difference in the United Kingdom is that general practitioner fundholders exist alongside health authorities and this means that to some degree there is competition between health authorities and fundholders. There is also competition among fundholders as different groups of general practitioners seek to demonstrate that they can purchase services more efficiently than others. Yet since the range of services purchased by fundholders and health authorities is usually different, competition between purchasers is more complex and limited than in the Netherlands and Germany. In these countries, the encouragement given to competition between insurers is an explicit and central objective of health care reform, even though it has yet to be implemented fully. What remains to be tested is whether in the process the risks involved in purchaser competition noted in Chapter 1 can be overcome.

There is much more common ground in the development of competition between providers. Competition evolved relatively rapidly in the United Kingdom, particularly in London and the major conurbations. The same applied in Stockholm where the number of acute hospitals in close proximity to each other offered a fertile environment for a market to be established. Provider competition developed more slowly in the Netherlands. This reflects the more cautious Dutch approach to health care reform, the limited scope for competition in many parts of the country and prevailing cultural characteristics. Insurers and providers have shown little interest in disrupting long established relationships, although this may change as the reforms move into the next phase. Similar observations apply to Germany where the encouragement given to sickness funds to contract selectively with providers is too recent to have had any major effects.

The contributors to this book offer a range of evidence to suggest that changes in the delivery of care have resulted from the reforms. Rehnberg, for example, describes how in Sweden productivity has increased and waiting times for treatment have fallen. Although similar changes also occurred in county councils that did not introduce fundamental reforms, the evidence indicates that the effects were greater in those that did. Van de Ven argues that, despite the slow pace of reform in the Netherlands, major changes have occurred in anticipation of a health care market developing. These include a stronger customer orientation, reductions in the price of some services, an investment in cost-accounting systems, and a plethora of initiatives designed to increase quality. Likewise, in the United Kingdom, the reforms have altered the balance of power within the NHS, involving a progressive shift from providers to purchasers, from doctors to managers and from hospital specialists to general practitioners. As in Sweden there is some evidence to suggest that productivity has increased and waiting times have fallen, and there has also been a refocusing on public health and primary care. What remains disputed is the extent of these changes and whether they would have occurred without the reforms. It has been suggested, for example, that increases to the NHS budget which accompanied the introduction of the reforms explain some of the gains that have been made, and that providing additional finance would have been a more effective way of tackling the problems facing the NHS than moving to a contract system.

The use of budgetary incentives to improve performance has met with mixed success. Not least, reforms that have sought to make money follow the patient have run into difficulties either because the incentives have led to the oversupply of services and therefore overspending of budgets (as has happened in Stockholm) or because money has not followed the patient and the weaknesses of global budgets persist (as in the United Kingdom).[11] In the process, the additional transaction costs involved in paying providers through contracts have become clear, especially in the United Kingdom. To date, at least, this appears to be less of a problem in Sweden – the only other country to have shifted from an integrated to a contract model. One of the reasons for this difference may be that Sweden invested heavily in information systems before separating purchaser and provider roles. On the other hand, both the United Kingdom and Sweden have largely escaped the additional transaction costs that arise when competing insurers use resources to advertise their products in the search for business.

More generally, the evidence from the United Kingdom and the United States indicates that the incentives contained within capitated budgets have an effect on clinical practice patterns. This is most apparent from the experience of HMOs and is reinforced by studies of general practitioner fundholding which show that fundholding has influenced the prescribing of pharmaceuticals and in some cases has resulted in more services being delivered in a primary care setting.[12] The German experience echoes that of the UK in showing that imposing budgets on doctors can reduce the cost of prescribing, although in this case it has been argued that the result has been to increase pressure elsewhere in the system.[13] In the case of fundholding, the United Kingdom experience indicates that not all general practitioners have changed their practices as a result of holding a budget and there is a continuing debate about whether the costs of fundholding outweigh the benefits.[14] Overall, experience suggests that incentives do influence providers' behaviour but they are difficult to control with precision and they produce unintended effects. This lends support to Morone's warning to beware of incentives:

> Although incentives are important for understanding problems and fashioning solutions, they are also tricky devils, always veering off in unanticipated ways. Give doctors incentives to be more efficient and they suddenly seek out healthy patients and spurn sick ones. Give farmers an incentive to plow under some of their land, and they grow more or less acreage. People are complicated, social systems almost infinitely so. A great many uninvited incentives lurk in each policy change.[15]

The contributors to this book have shown that in pursuing the goal of competition, policy makers have not abandoned planning and regulation. Rather, the aim has been to combine some market incentives with a framework of rules to guide competition and the capacity to intervene to tackle problems when they arise. The reforms are therefore best described as leading to the establishment of regulated or managed markets. Indeed, the experience reported in earlier chapters suggests that the phrase 'politically managed market' is a more apt description of the path that reform has taken. The key factor here is that in view of the well known market failures in health care, effective regulation is essential and politicians cannot distance themselves from such regulation when public finance accounts for the bulk of health services expenditure. The effect has been to weaken the strength of the incentives that have been introduced and in some cases to force politicians to have second thoughts about the wisdom of competitive strategies.

This has been most apparent in Sweden and the United Kingdom where politicians have placed less emphasis recently in their public pronouncements on competition and have argued instead for greater cooperation between purchasers and providers. Similar trends are evident in the Netherlands. Some of the reasons for this are identified by Saltman in an assessment of the lessons that have emerged from market-oriented reforms.[16] As Saltman notes, it appears that competition has a greater role to play in relation to service provision than health insurance. Yet even in the case of service provision, reforms have been harder to implement than expected, and competition has provoked opposition from both health service staff and the public. Furthermore, as Saltman, Maynard and others have observed, the regulatory frameworks used in managed markets are often incomplete or contradictory, producing unforeseen consequences.[17] Implementation has been affected too by the emergence of conflicts between objectives such as efficiency and effectiveness, and negotiated contracts and patient choice.

If the separation of purchaser and provider roles within the contract model remains but the emphasis on competition has been reduced, then the reforms that have been introduced are being used for other purposes. In particular, the language of accountability is replacing that of markets with contract systems being seen mainly as a way of making transparent the use of resources. This has always been the case in Sweden where geography has acted as a constraint on competition outside urban areas but it is also apparent in the United Kingdom and Netherlands. Yet far from leading to a return to the integrated model, disillusion with markets is provoking new thinking on how the institutional changes that have occurred can be used for other purposes. Recognizing the weaknesses of the old centralized, command-and-control systems, including the problem of provider capture, lack of responsiveness to users and few incentives for efficiency, analysts have argued the need to develop a contract based model in which purchasers and providers work together in long-term relationships but where the option always exists for a purchaser to move a contract if other methods of improving performance are not effective. Such an approach has been described as 'contestability' to distinguish it from both planned approaches to health care financing and delivery and those based on competition.[18] The process of reform therefore resembles the Hegelian dialectic with a new synthesis emerging out of the ashes of previous policies.

To return to Chapter 1, who have been the winners and losers and what have been the distributional effects? It is this question that is most difficult to answer because of the absence of systematic evaluation. While some studies suggest that equity may have been sacrificed in the pursuit of efficiency and responsiveness, more work is needed to establish whether this is generally the case. Furthermore, even assuming that equity has been sacrificed, the way in which this has happened needs to be described more precisely. Indeed, given that equity was in any case an elusive goal in the unreformed health care systems described in this book, the balance sheet that is drawn up to describe the impact of the reforms has to be clear about the starting point of different systems as well as the consequence of the policies pursued. In this context, it is pertinent to recall Rehnberg's observation that in Sweden there is no evidence that equity has been undermined by market-oriented reforms within a publicly financed system. One of the reasons for this may be the importance attached to equity in Sweden over a long period of time and its resilience in the face of alternative values.

On the basis of our analysis, it is difficult to escape the conclusion that the failure to evaluate the reforms that have been pursued is a major missed opportunity. Despite calls for policy (as well as medicine) to be evidence based, there has been a dearth of proper evaluations and this has compounded the tendency of policy makers to jump on the reform bandwagon.[19] Not only this, but also promising early reports of the impact of reforms, often based on incomplete data, may have given a misleading impression of the policies that were pursued. When allied to the influence exerted by prestigious international organizations, the effect was to encourage the dissemination of bad or at best half good policies.[20] To be sure, politics is concerned with decision making in conditions of considerable uncertainty, and policy makers cannot wait until the definitive results of evaluative studies are available. Nevertheless, with the benefit of hindsight, and to be fair this point was made at the genesis of many reform efforts, more could and should have been done to study the impact of the strategies that were pursued.

THE NEW REFORM AGENDA

Disillusion with competition has been associated with a further phase of reform in which policy makers have launched a series of initiatives even in advance of conclusive evidence about the impact of earlier reforms.[21] For example, there is concern to balance the focus on health service efficiency and responsiveness with greater attention to the influences on health which occur outside the health sector. Stimulated by the WHO's *Health for All by the Year 2000* initiative,[22] and by mounting evidence that the major causes of premature death and disability are to be found in the social and economic environment and in people's behaviour and lifestyles, a number of countries have adopted national health strategies. This includes giving priority to the prevention of ill health, health promotion, and public health. It also encompasses setting targets for health improvement at the population level. A further strand in this debate is the encouragement given to healthy public policies to ensure that action in fields such as housing, education and transport contribute to health improvement.

Linked to the renewed interest in public health, policy makers have sought to give greater priority to primary care and alternatives to hospital based medicine. This is in part because programmes of health promotion are often delivered within primary care and in part because advances in health care technology have facilitated a shift in the site of service provision out of hospitals and into the community. With a wider range of services being provided by primary care physicians and their colleagues, there is increasing emphasis on initiatives such as fundholding and HMOs as instruments for accelerating this trend. Indeed, the emergence of primary managed care organizations, in which general practitioners work within a budget to either provide or procure necessary medical services for their patients and do so within a framework of guidelines on the prevention and treatment of illness, appears to be an issue of growing importance for the future.[23] A key feature of these organizations is the use of budgetary incentives to encourage the cost effective delivery of services. These initiatives in effect combine elements of the three strategies of reform identified in Chapter 1 – the use of market-like mechanisms, policies to strengthen the management of health services and the development of budgetary incentives to improve performance – in an attempt to go beyond the scope of existing reform programmes.

What remains unclear is how primary managed care organizations will relate to the providers of hospital and specialist services. Reviewing developments in California, Robinson and Casalino note how a highly competitive market has stimulated the expansion of managed care, centred on groups of primary care physicians.[24] In some cases these groups have joined with hospitals in vertically integrated organizations; in others they have retained their independence but have established links with specialists through 'virtual integration'. As Robinson and Casalino observe, what began as a revolution in health care financing is in this way leading to a major change in health care organization. These developments are mirrored in the United Kingdom where the NHS reforms have led groups of fundholders and non-fundholders to explore ways in which primary care and secondary care can be more closely integrated.

As in the United States, a range of models have emerged. Increased collaboration between general practitioners within primary care exists alongside opportunities for competition between groups of doctors for patients and resources.[25] In the longer term, this could lead to the establishment of multi-specialist groups of physicians, and indeed to the development of NHS trusts encompassing primary care as well as hospital and community health services. Equally, general practitioners may prefer to keep their distance from hospitals and specialists and contract with them as necessary. If this were to happen, the kind of virtual integration described by Robinson and Casalino would prevail over vertical integration. Whatever the outcome, reforms to the delivery of health care on both sides of the Atlantic are characterized by a focus on primary care and the use of primary care physicians to manage the use of secondary care services. Given the rapid pace of change, it is difficult to predict where these developments will lead and whether, as we have noted in the case of competition, there will be a reaction in which secondary care issues return to the centre of the agenda.

Even more fundamentally, attention is turning to an examination of the scope of publicly financed health care and a debate about what should be in the health benefits package.[26] The state of Oregon has led the way in this debate by establishing a health services commission to advise on priorities for the Medicaid programme. Following a lengthy process of analysis and debate, in 1994 it was agreed that 565 treatments out of a total of almost 700 would be funded. By excluding some low priority services from coverage, Oregon was able to extend Medicaid to groups in the population who were previously deemed ineligible because they failed the means test for this programme. Explicit discussions of health care priority setting have also occurred in New Zealand where the government established a committee in 1992 to make recommendations on the core services to be included in the New Zealand health service.[27] The committee concluded that this task was best approached not by drawing up a list of exclusions Oregon-style but rather by making an overall assessment of priorities and by examining individual services in depth. The latter objective was pursued using consensus conferences. Drawing on the results of these conferences, the core services committee formulated guidance on priorities and levels of service provision. Services examined in this way include joint replacement and heart surgery.

The United Kingdom government has so far resisted calls to set up a national committee to review priorities in the NHS, despite increasing evidence that some patients are being denied treatment and that there is a growing gap between demand and supply. Instead, in response to a report produced by a parliamentary committee, the government argued that there was no need to ration core services and that priority should be given to ensuring that resources were used cost-effectively.[28] To help health authorities and fundholders in this task, support has been given to the production of bulletins summarizing evidence on particular medical conditions, and health authorities have been encouraged to develop clinical guidelines and protocols in collaboration with providers. The NHS research and development programme also includes a major commitment to health technology assessment. As in New Zealand, excluding services from the NHS menu has been rejected by health ministers who have taken the view that the main need is to eliminate ineffective service provision and ensure that effective services are delivered appropriately.

One of the most sophisticated examples of priority setting is in the Netherlands. The report of the Dunning Committee, set up to advise on the basic benefits package to be funded in the Dutch social insurance system, set out a framework for thinking about these issues making use of four criteria.[29] These involved asking whether the service or treatment concerned was necessary from the community's point of view, whether it was effective and efficient, and whether it could be left to personal responsibility. Applying these criteria to particular examples, the committee concluded that *in vitro* fertilization should be excluded because it was not necessary to fund this from public sources from the community's point of view. The committee also recommended that dental care for adults should be excluded because it could be left to personal responsibility. In parallel, and providing a bridge between the Oregon and New Zealand approaches to priority setting, a strong emphasis was placed on drawing up guidelines for the provision of services in the benefits package. This was intended to ensure that these services were provided effectively and appropriately.

A rather different approach has been pursued in Sweden. Drawing on earlier work in Norway, an expert committee set up by the Swedish government identified a number of broad priorities at both the political and clinical levels of decision making.[30] The committee then went on to identify the values or principles that should guide priority setting. Three principles were enunciated: human dignity, need or solidarity and efficiency. Furthermore, in applying the efficiency principle, the committee argued that this should be used only for comparing alternative ways of treating the same condition, not for comparing treatments of different conditions. In other words, they rejected the use of techniques such as cost per quality adjusted life years which have been advocated by economists as a way of setting priorities across the range of service provision. The committee was also clear in the view that criteria such as age and income were not relevant in determining priorities.

These examples have been chosen because policy makers in Oregon, New Zealand, the United Kingdom, the Netherlands, Sweden and Norway have shown a particular interest in priority setting. Yet in a situation in which the demand for health care continues to rise because of demographic pressures, advances in medical science and rising public expectations, and when public resources are subject to tight controls, policy makers everywhere are having to reassess the commitment to universal population coverage and comprehensive service provision. To some degree, this can be seen as the price to be paid for earlier success in containing costs at the macro level. At the time of writing, there has been no significant retreat from the principles of universality and comprehensiveness, and the difficulties of defining a set of core services to be funded through public sources has become increasingly apparent. It is for this reason that attention has focused on clarifying the values and principles that should guide priority setting and the processes that might help to legitimize decisions. Policy makers have also concentrated on ensuring that resources are used cost effectively and have sought to involve health care professionals and the public in debating priorities.

It is this that lies behind the renewed interest in health technology assessment and evidence based medicine. Given that new technologies tend to increase overall costs by opening up new opportunities for diagnosis and treatment, this issue is receiving increasing attention.[31] Major initiatives have been launched in this field in a number of countries and there is increasing international cooperation through the Cochrane Collaboration and related projects. In view of widespread variations in clinical practice patterns, and evidence that technologies have often been adopted in the past in the absence of evidence of effectiveness, the priority attached to health technology assessment is seen by many analysts as holding the key to the health care dilemma of demand exceeding supply. Others are more doubtful about the claims made for health technology assessment, questioning the basis of the 'new scientism' in health care and pointing to the inevitable uncertainties in medical practice as a barrier to the more systematic use of evidence in action.[32] As yet, this has not deterred the enthusiasts and a significant investment continues to be made in this area.

What these comments illustrate is the constantly changing nature of the health care reform debate. While this book has focused on experience up to 1996, already new issues and initiatives are emerging. Although some of these initiatives may prove short lived, nevertheless further layers of complexity have been added to the already convoluted pattern of health care reform. If health policy in the late 1970s and early 1980s was dominated by concern to achieve cost containment at the macro level, and in the late 1980s and early 1990s focused on measures to increase efficiency and enhance responsiveness at the micro level, then in the mid-1990s attention has turned to the cost effectiveness of health care and the difficult choices involved in setting priorities. Figure 7.1 summarizes the different phases of health care reform and the main themes that have arisen during each phase. It is a safe prediction that the interest shown in priority setting will grow in importance with the

PHASE ONE:	Late 1970s/early 1980s
THEME:	Cost containment at the macro level
POLICY INSTRUMENTS:	Prospective global budgets for hospitals
	Controls over hospital building and the acquisition of medical equipment
	Limits on doctors' fees and incomes
	Restrictions on the numbers undertaking education and training
PHASE TWO:	Late 1980s/early 1990s
THEME:	Micro efficiency and responsiveness to users
POLICY INSTRUMENTS:	Market-like mechanisms
	Management reforms
	Budgetary incentives
PHASE THREE:	Late 1990s
THEME:	Rationing and priority setting
POLICY INSTRUMENTS:	Public health
	Primary care
	Managed care
	Health technology assessment
	Evidence based medicine

Figure 7.1 Phases in health care reform

passage of time. As in the use for policy instruments to increase efficiency and enhance responsiveness, the search for a holy grail is likely to prove fruitless. Choices in health care are inherently difficult and reflect the values that prevail in particular health systems. Each country will therefore have to seek its own solution, recognizing that there are no technical fixes and that a strategic approach is needed to deal with the complexities involved.

CONCLUSION

In summary, it can be suggested that the following lessons have emerged from experience so far:

• the United States system fails to meet basic social goals and at the macro level contains few lessons for Europeans – except to ignore claims that the United States approach should be copied in Europe;

- there has been a shift from the public integrated model to the public contract model in the United Kingdom and parts of Sweden. In the Netherlands and Germany, the aim has been to transform insurers from relatively passive payers to discriminating and prudent purchasers;
- market-like mechanisms have been widely introduced, although planning and regulation have not been abandoned. Policy makers have favoured managed markets and politicians have continued to be closely involved in steering the development of health services;
- greater emphasis has been given to provider competition than competition between purchasers although the latter is an explicit and central objective of health care reform in the Netherlands and Germany;
- the importance of the purchaser role was not fully appreciated at the outset of recent reforms and only latterly has action been taken to rectify this;
- patient choice has been a key feature of health care reform. This includes giving priority to the reduction of waiting lists by establishing targets and guarantees;
- the extent of convergence in health care reform should not be exaggerated. Although the vocabulary of reform may be international, the words used mean different things in different systems and there are important differences of emphasis;
- the use of budgetary incentives has met with mixed success. Incentives do appear to influence the behaviour of providers but they are difficult to control with precision and may produce unintended effects;
- the reforms that have been pursued have had a number of effects, both positive and negative. These include a renewed emphasis on efficiency, greater attention to quality, and changes in the relationship between different actors. There is some evidence that equity may have suffered and that transaction costs have increased, but this is more apparent in the United Kingdom than elsewhere;
- the distributional effects – who wins and who loses – are largely unknown because of the absence of systematic evaluation. The failure to rigorously evaluate the reforms that have been introduced is a major missed opportunity;
- policy makers in some countries are moving away from competitive strategies and are placing greater emphasis on accountability and contestability. This does not entail a return to the integrated model but rather a search for a synthesis of different approaches;

- even in advance of conclusive evidence about the effects of earlier reforms, new policy initiatives are emerging on to the agenda. These include priority for public health, primary care and alternatives to hospital based medicine. The emergence of managed care organizations is a key element in this process;
- more fundamentally, a debate is opening up about the scope of publicly financed health care and the rationing of health services. This has not yet led to the widespread exclusion of services from public funding and instead the emphasis has been placed on achieving greater cost effectiveness in the use of resources through health technology assessment and evidence based medicine.

These lessons suggest that it is important to approach the reform of health care financing and delivery with a degree of humility about our understanding of the effectiveness of different strategies. As we have seen, it is easier to describe the changes that are occurring than to assess their effects. A number of negative lessons do emerge from experience but good practices supported by hard evidence are more difficult to identify. For these reasons, it is necessary to be cautious before introducing changes which are untried and untested. Analysts who 'take a view' on the path that reform should take need to be explicit about the basis on which they formulate their recommendations and the extent to which these recommendations are supported by the available facts.[33] This is not to suggest that change should never occur, rather that a pragmatic approach is called for in which there is a commitment to evaluation and learning from experience. This includes making an investment in learning from the experience of others. As *The Economist* has commented:

> Most countries are dealing with health-care reform as if each was on Mars. Few have tried to learn from others. . . . This indifference to the international face of doctoring is a huge mistake . . . there are lessons to be learnt from looking at different ways of paying for and delivering the goods. Instead of each country trying out its own experiments, they should be studying each other's for ideas and pitfalls.[34]

Although some progress has recently been made in sharing the results of international experience, much remains to be done, and further studies are needed to assist in the dissemination of experience.

NOTES

1 R. Klein (1995) Big bang health care reform – Does it work?: The case of Britain's 1991 National Health Service reforms. *The Milbank Quarterly*, 73 (3): 299–337.

2 C.J. Ham (1994) Where now for the NHS reforms? *British Medical Journal*, 309: 351–2.

3 On this point see P. Pierson (1994) *Dismantling the Welfare State?* Cambridge: Cambridge University Press.

4 This section draws on various sources including J. Appleby and C.J. Ham (1995) 'The future of health and health care services', report to Healthcare 2000. London: Shire Hall; and C.J. Ham and M. Brommels (1994) Health care reform in the Netherlands, Sweden and the United Kingdom. *Health Affairs*, 13 (4): 106–19.

5 W.C. Hsiao (1994) 'Marketization' – The illusory magic pill. *Health Economics*, 3: 355.

6 R. Evans, A. Maynard, A. Prekker and U. Reinhardt (1994) Health care reforms. *Health Economics*, 3: 359.

7 OECD (1992) *The Reform of Health Care: A Comparative Analysis of Seven OECD Countries*. Paris: Organisation for Economic Cooperation and Development; OECD (1994) *The Reform of Health Care Systems: A Review of Seventeen OECD Countries*. Paris: Organisation for Economic Cooperation and Development.

8 C.J. Ham, R. Robinson and M. Benzeval (1990) *Health Check*. London: King's Fund Institute.

9 J.C. Robinson (1995) Health care purchasing and market changes in California. *Health Affairs*, 14 (4): 117–30.

10 C.J. Ham (1996) Population-centred and patient-focused purchasing: the UK experience. *The Milbank Quarterly*, 74 (2): 191–214.

11 C.J. Ham and M. Brommels (1994) Health care reform in the Netherlands, Sweden and the United Kingdom. *Health Affairs*, 13 (4): 106–19.

12 H.S. Luft (1994) Health maintenance organisations: Is the United States' experience applicable elsewhere? in OECD (ed.) *Health: Quality and Choice*. Paris: Organisation for Economic Cooperation and Development; H. Glennerster, M. Matsaganis and P. Owens with S. Hancock (1994) *Implementing GP Fundholding*. Buckingham: Open University Press.

13 R. Busse and C. Howorth (1996) Fixed budgets in the pharmaceutical sector in Germany: Effects on cost and quality, in F.W. Schwartz, H. Glennerster and R. B. Saltman (eds) *Fixing Health Budgets*. Chichester: John Wiley.

14 Audit Commission (1996) *What the Doctor Ordered*. London: HMSO.

15 J.A. Morone (1986) Seven laws of policy analysis. *Journal of Policy Analysis and Management*, 5 (4): 817–19.

16 R. Saltman (1994) A conceptual overview of recent health care reforms. *European Journal of Public Health*, 4: 287–93.

17 A. Maynard (1994) Can competition enhance efficiency in health care? Lessons from the reforms of the UK National Health Service. *Social Science and Medicine*, 39 (10): 1433–45.

18 C.J. Ham (1996) Contestability: A middle path for health care. *British Medical Journal*, 312: 70–1; see also C.J. Ham (1996) *Beyond Planning and Markets: The Future of the National Health Service*. London: DEMOS.

19 C.J. Ham, D.J. Hunter and R. Robinson (1995) Evidence based policy making. *British Medical Journal*, 310: 71–2.

20 For example, OECD (1994) *OECD Economic Surveys: United Kingdom*. Paris: Organisation for Economic Cooperation and Development, and the critique of this by K. Bloor and A. Maynard (1994) An outsider's view of the NHS reforms. *British Medical Journal*, 309: 352–3.

21 OECD (1995) *New Directions in Health Care Policy*. Paris: Organisation for Economic Cooperation and Development.

22 WHO (1985) *Health for All by the Year 2000*. Copenhagen: WHO.

23 B. Robinson (1996) Primary managed care: The Lyme alternative, in G. Meads (ed.) *Future Options for General Practice*. Oxford: Radcliffe Medical Press.

24 J.C. Robinson and L.P. Casalino (1996) Vertical integration and organisational networks in health care. *Health Affairs*, 15 (1): 7–22.

25 C.J. Ham (1996) A primary care market? *British Medical Journal*, 313: 127–8.

26 F. Honigsbaum, J. Calltorp, C.J. Ham and S. Holmstrom (1995) *Priority Setting Processes for Healthcare*. Oxford: Radcliffe Medical Press.

27 National Advisory Committee (1992) *Core Services 1993/1994*. Wellington: National Advisory Committee.

28 House of Commons Health Committee (1995) *Priority Setting in the NHS*. London: HMSO; Department of Health (1995) *Government Response to the First Report of the Health Committee Session 1994–95*. London: HMSO.

29 Government Committee on Choices in Health Care (1992) *Choices in Health Care*. Rijswijk: Ministry of Welfare, Health and Cultural Affairs.

30 Health Care and Medical Priorities Commission (1992) *No Easy Choices: the Difficult Priorities of Health Care*. Stockholm: Ministry of Health and Social Affairs.

31 H. Aaron (1996) Thinking about health care finance: some propositions, in OECD (ed.) *Health Care Reforms. The Will to Change*. Paris: Organisation for Economic Cooperation and Development.

32 R. Klein, P. Day and S. Redmayne (1996) *Managing Scarcity*. Buckingham: Open University Press.

33 For example, see OECD (1995) *New Directions in Health Care Policy*. Paris: Organisation of Economic Cooperation and Development.

34 *The Economist* (1991) Surgery needed: A survey of health care, 6–12 July.

INDEX

References in italic indicate figures or tables.
Abbreviations:
Ger. = Germany
Neth. = Netherlands
Sw. = Sweden
UK = United Kingdom
US = United States

IMPLEMENTING PLANNED MARKETS IN HEALTH CARE
BALANCING SOCIAL AND ECONOMIC RESPONSIBILITY

Richard B. Saltman and Casten von Otter (eds)

- What lessons can be learned from the health reform process to date?
- What direction will future health reforms take in the industrialized world?

Implementing Planned Markets in Health Care brings together an international team of experts to address these important questions. Drawing on experiences in Northern Europe and the United States, it examines the key concepts behind the present push toward health reform in the industrialized world:

- contracting and solidarity
- contestable v. competitive markets
- the role of vouchers
- physicians' clinical autonomy

Also included are case studies of planned market approaches based on contracts, patient choice, and on quality of care. The book concludes with a broad comparative assessment of the main themes and points towards the most likely developments in future *planned market* models of health care.

Contents
Introduction – Part 1: The politics of contracting – Contracting and the purchaser-provider split – Contracting and solidarity – Regulation of planned markets in health care – Contracting and political boards in planned markets – Part 2: Balancing incentives and accountability – Costs, productivity and financial outcomes of managed care – Vouchers in planned markets – Clinical autonomy and planned markets – Part 3: Constructing entrepreneurial providers – Self-governing trusts and GP fundholders – Implementing planned markets in health services – Competitive hospital markets based on quality – Part 4: Conclusion – Index.

Contributors
Anders Anell, Göran Arvidsson, Mats Brommels, Aad A. de Roo, Stephen Harrison, Nancy M. Kane, Christian M. Koeck, Julian Le Grand, Britta Neugaard, Ray Robinson, Richard B. Saltman, Clive H. Smee, Casten von Otter.

272pp   0 335 19425 7 (Paperback)   0 335 19426 5 (Hardback)